D1076211

EYEWITNESS VISUAL DICTIONARIES

THE VISUAL
DICTIONARY *of the*
HORSE

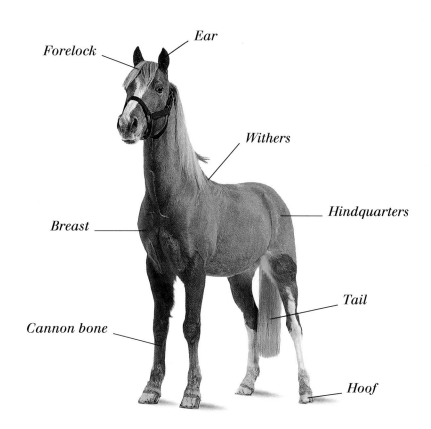

Forelock

Ear

Withers

Hindquarters

Breast

Tail

Cannon bone

Hoof

**EXTERNAL FEATURES
OF A HORSE**

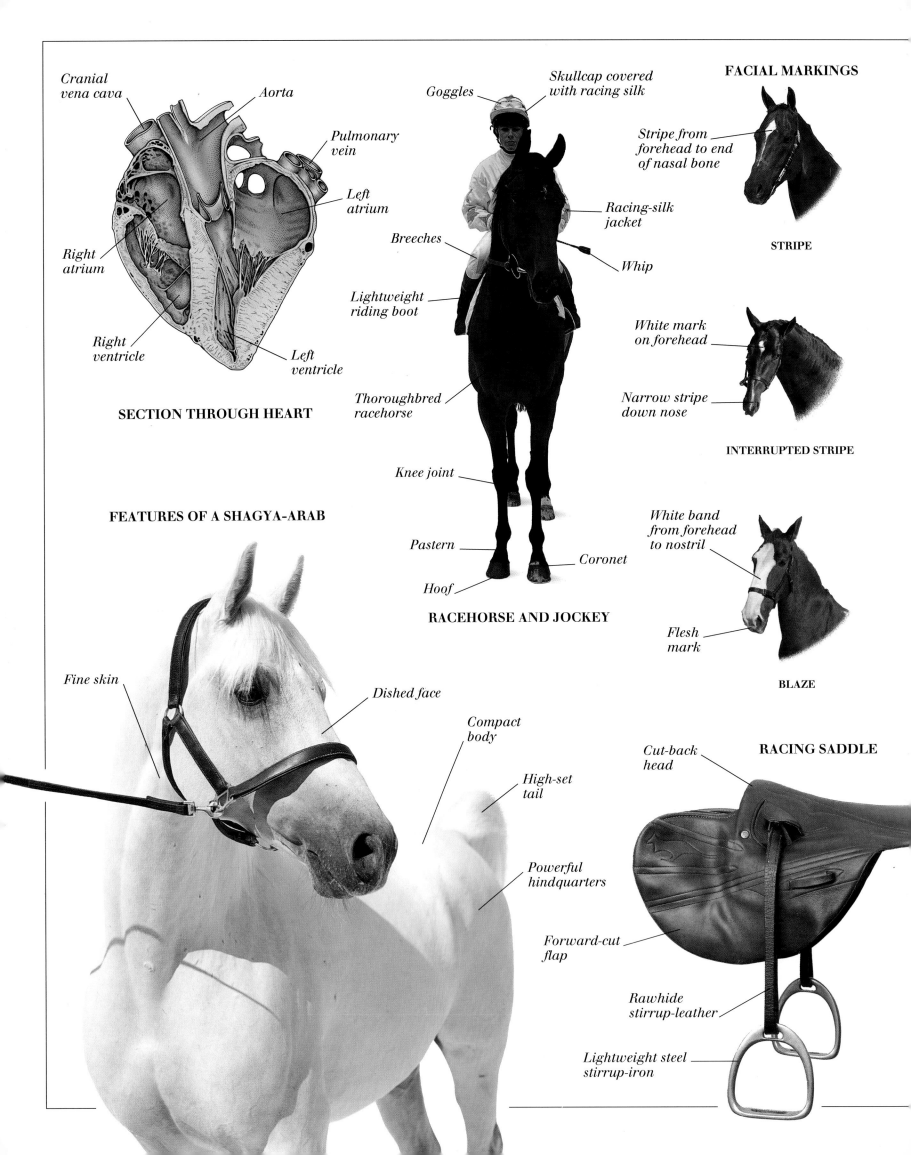

SECTION THROUGH HEART

Cranial vena cava

Aorta

Pulmonary vein

Left atrium

Right atrium

Right ventricle

Left ventricle

FACIAL MARKINGS

Stripe from forehead to end of nasal bone

STRIPE

White mark on forehead

Narrow stripe down nose

INTERRUPTED STRIPE

Goggles

Skullcap covered with racing silk

Racing-silk jacket

Breeches

Whip

Lightweight riding boot

Thoroughbred racehorse

Knee joint

Pastern

Coronet

Hoof

RACEHORSE AND JOCKEY

White band from forehead to nostril

Flesh mark

BLAZE

FEATURES OF A SHAGYA-ARAB

Fine skin

Dished face

Compact body

High-set tail

Powerful hindquarters

RACING SADDLE

Cut-back head

Forward-cut flap

Rawhide stirrup-leather

Lightweight steel stirrup-iron

EYEWITNESS VISUAL DICTIONARIES

THE VISUAL
DICTIONARY *of the*
HORSE

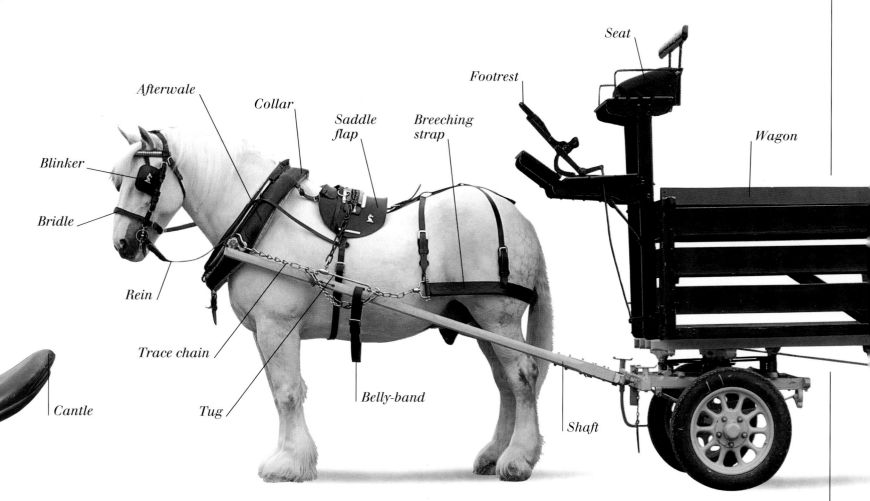

Seat

Footrest

Afterwale

Collar

Saddle flap

Breeching strap

Wagon

Blinker

Bridle

Rein

Trace chain

Tug

Belly-band

Shaft

Cantle

HORSE HARNESSED TO WAGON

Stoddart

A DORLING KINDERSLEY BOOK

Art Editor Paul Calver
Design Assistant Susan Knight

Project Editor Louise Tucker
Consultant Editors Dr Juliet Clutton-Brock, Sarah Morgan

Managing Art Editor Philip Gilderdale
Senior Editor Martyn Page
Managing Editor Ruth Midgley

Illustrators Dan Wright, Tony Graham, Joanna Cameron
Production Jayne Simpson

Powerful neck
Broad, powerful chest

Yellowish-red coat
Black mane

Powerful hindquarters
Straight profile

Compact body
Well-defined withers

Low withers
Small head

ARDENNAIS   LUSITANO   BRETON   ANGLO-ARAB   DARTMOOR PONY

EXAMPLES OF HORSE BREEDS

First published in Canada in 1994 by Stoddart Publishing Co. Limited
34 Lesmill Road, Toronto, Canada, M3B 2T6
Reprinted 1995
Published in Great Britain in 1994
by Dorling Kindersley Limited, 9 Henrietta Street, London WC2E 8PS, England

Copyright © 1994 Dorling Kindersley Limited, London

All rights reserved. No part of this publication may be
reproduced or transmitted in any form or by any means, electronic or
mechanical, including photocopy, recording or any information storage and
retrieval system, without permission in writing from the publisher.

Canadian Cataloguing in Publication Data
Main entry under title:
The Visual dictionary of the horse
(Eyewitness visual dictionaries)
Includes index.
ISBN 0-7737-2783-3

1. Horses - Dictionaries, Juvenile.
2. Picture dictionaries, English - Juvenile literature. I. Series.
English - Juvenile literature. I. Series.

SF278.V57 1994   j636.1'003   C93-095331-2

Reproduced by Colourscan, Singapore
Printed and bound by Arnoldo Mondadori, Verona, Italy

Contents

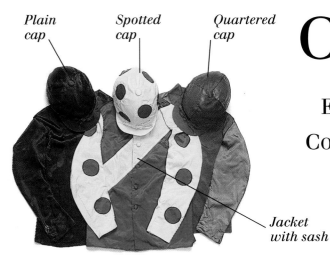

Plain cap

Spotted cap

Quartered cap

Jacket with sash

RACING SILKS

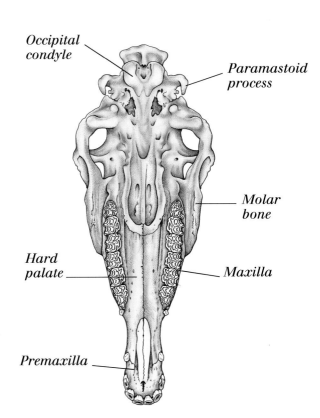

Long, wavy mane

Strong, sloping shoulders

ANDALUCIAN

Occipital condyle

Paramastoid process

Molar bone

Hard palate

Maxilla

Premaxilla

UPPER JAW OF SKULL FROM BELOW

Short face

Small mouth

Short, small body

Wide-based stance for stability

Long, thin limbs

NEWBORN FOAL

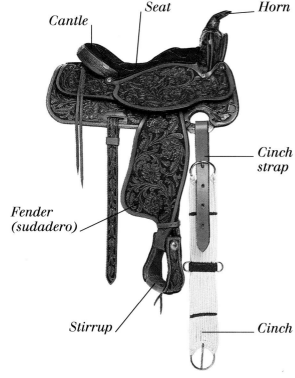

Rider leans forwards in saddle

Horse with all four legs raised

GALLOPING

Cantle

Seat

Horn

Fender (sudadero)

Cinch strap

Stirrup

Cinch

WESTERN SADDLE

External features

ALTHOUGH THE APPEARANCE OF MODERN HORSES varies enormously among breeds, all horses are descended from ancestral wild horses. It has been the process of selective breeding over hundreds of years that has led to the great variations among the many breeds. Now, most breeds of horse fall into one of three categories: ponies, light horses, or heavy horses. Breeds are divided into these categories by differences in weight, gait, colour, body build and proportion, and height. A horse's height is the distance from the highest point of the withers to the ground. It is traditionally measured in hands, based on the approximate width of a man's hand: four inches (about 10 cm). Light horses are chiefly differentiated from heavy horses by body build and proportion. Ponies are usually differentiated from all other horses by height; ponies are less than 14.2 hands (147 cm) high. Despite the differences between breeds, all horses have certain physical features in common, known as points. The points of a horse are the visible external features, such as the tail and ears, as well as the parts of the skeleton and the superficial muscles that can be felt through the skin, such as the facial crest and jugular groove.

TYPES OF HORSE

PONY
Height range: 10–14.2 hands
(102–147 cm)

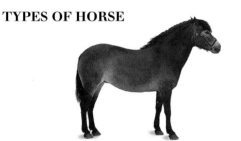

LIGHT HORSE
Height range: 14.2–17.2 hands
(147–178 cm)

HEAVY HORSE
Height range: 14.2–18 hands
(147–183 cm)

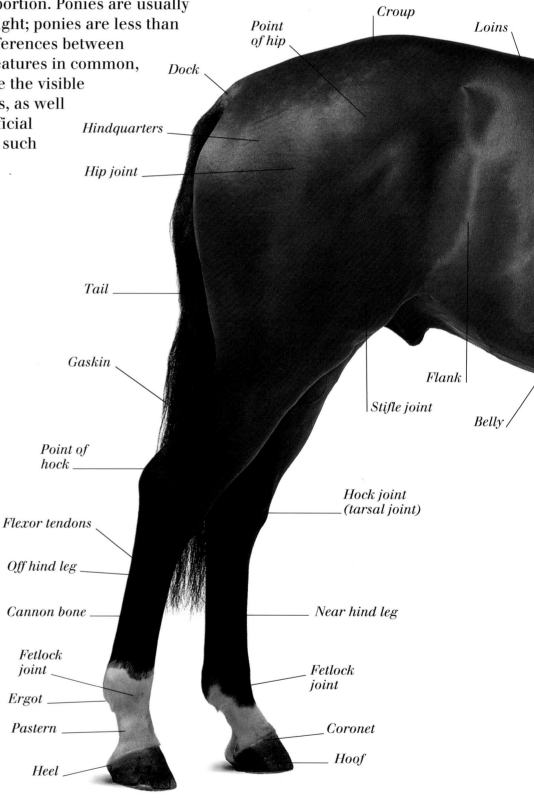

Point of hip

Croup

Loins

Dock

Hindquarters

Hip joint

Tail

Gaskin

Flank

Stifle joint

Belly

Point of hock

Hock joint
(tarsal joint)

Flexor tendons

Off hind leg

Cannon bone

Near hind leg

Fetlock joint

Fetlock joint

Ergot

Pastern

Coronet

Hoof

Heel

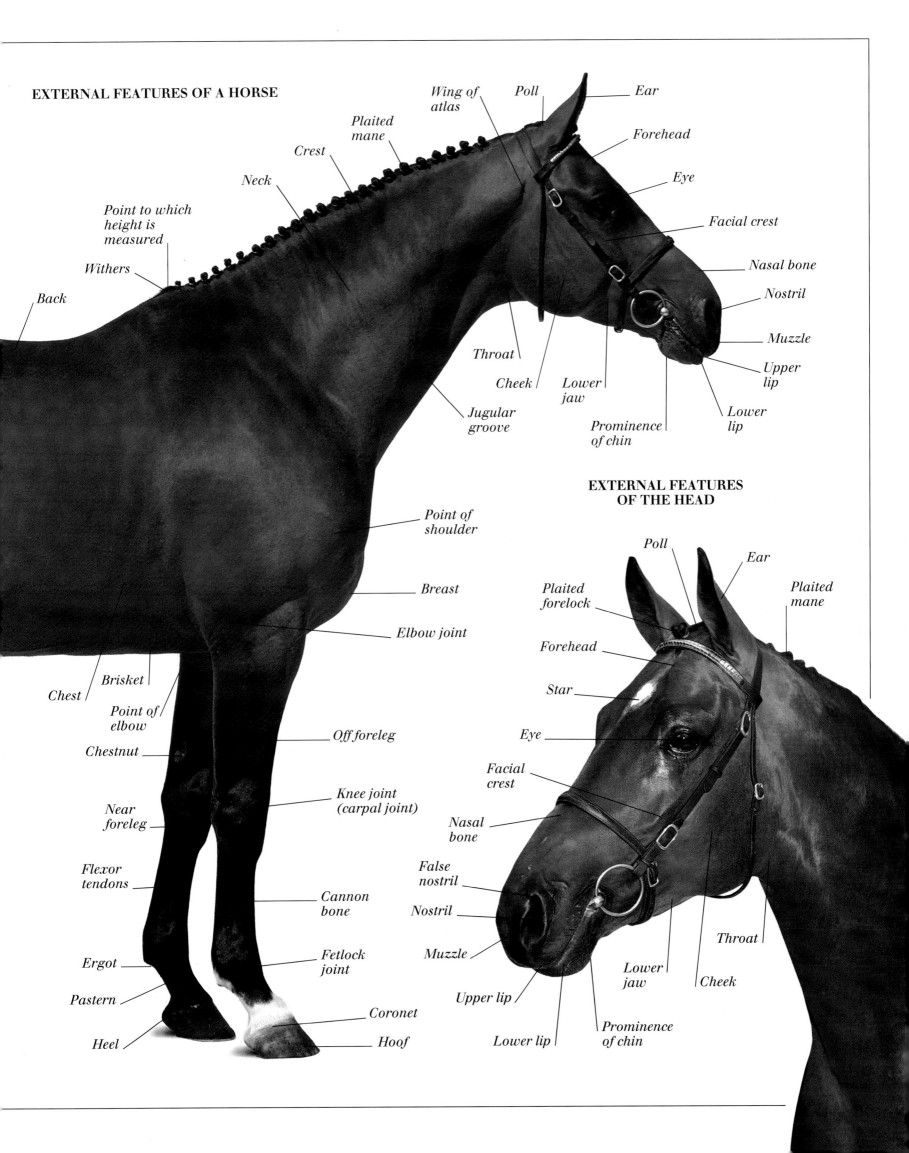

EXTERNAL FEATURES OF A HORSE

Wing of atlas

Poll

Ear

Plaited mane

Forehead

Crest

Eye

Neck

Facial crest

Point to which height is measured

Nasal bone

Withers

Nostril

Back

Muzzle

Throat

Upper lip

Cheek

Lower jaw

Lower lip

Jugular groove

Prominence of chin

EXTERNAL FEATURES OF THE HEAD

Point of shoulder

Poll

Ear

Plaited forelock

Plaited mane

Breast

Forehead

Elbow joint

Star

Eye

Facial crest

Chest

Brisket

Nasal bone

Point of elbow

False nostril

Chestnut

Off foreleg

Nostril

Knee joint (carpal joint)

Muzzle

Throat

Near foreleg

Upper lip

Lower jaw

Cheek

Flexor tendons

Cannon bone

Lower lip

Prominence of chin

Ergot

Fetlock joint

Pastern

Coronet

Heel

Hoof

Colours and markings

ALL PRESENT-DAY DOMESTIC HORSES are descended from dun-coloured wild horses. Dun horses typically have a yellowish-red or light reddish-brown main coat colour with a dark mane and tail. Today, selective breeding has produced a range of horse colours, such as bay, chestnut, and grey. Most horse colours are defined by the coat alone, although some are distinguished by a combination of the coat colour with specific mane and tail colours. For example, a Palomino horse has a gold coat with a white mane and tail. Some breeds are selectively bred to be one particular colour, so the Friesian horse is always black. Combinations of colour on the coat also have special terms, so a dapple-grey coat has small dark grey rings on a paler grey base. The white markings on the face and limbs have particular names. For example, a white patch on the forehead is known as a star, and white hair reaching up to the knee or hock is called a stocking marking.

STAR

STRIPE

BLAZE

WHITE FACE

INTERRUPTED STRIPE

SNIP

PONY WITH DORSAL STRIPE

Chestnut mane

Chestnut tail

White face

Grey mane

Dark grey rings on light grey base

Grey tail

Large white patches on another base colour (here chestnut)

Stocking marking

COLOUR: DAPPLE-GREY
Breed: Orlov Trotter

COLOUR: SKEWBALD
Breed: Pinto

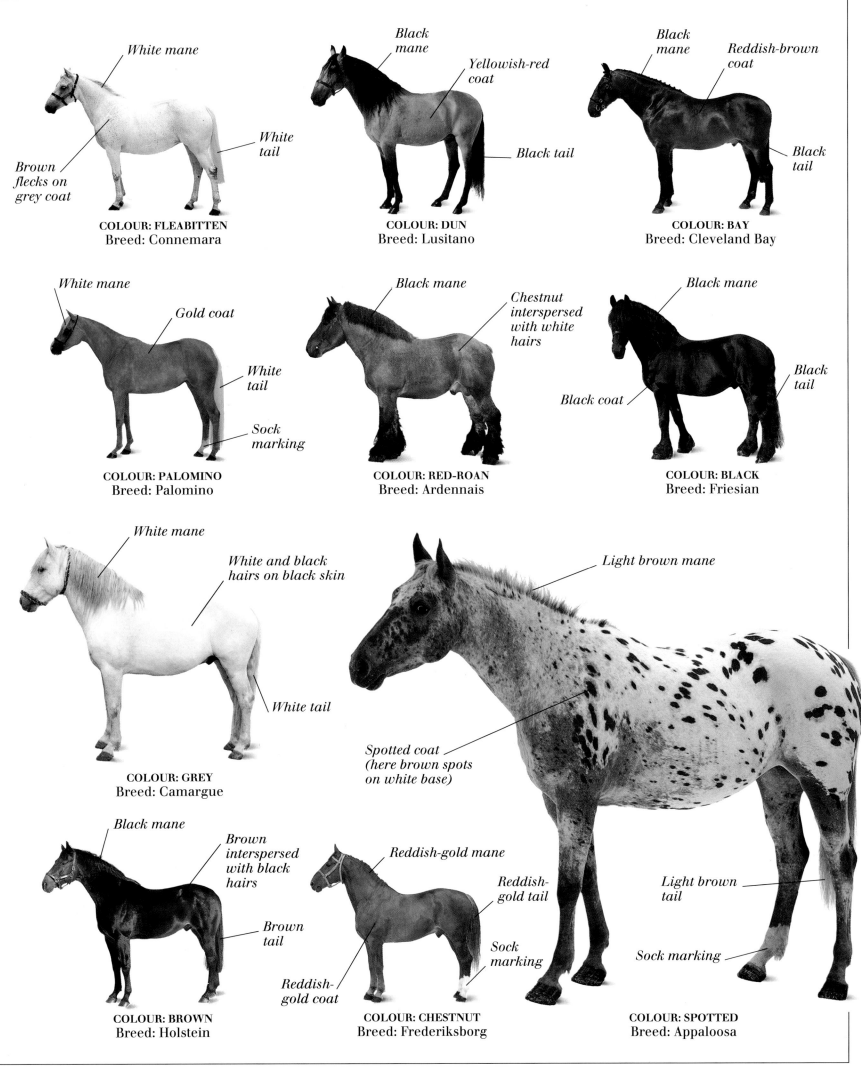

White mane

Brown flecks on grey coat

White tail

COLOUR: FLEABITTEN
Breed: Connemara

Black mane

Yellowish-red coat

Black tail

COLOUR: DUN
Breed: Lusitano

Black mane

Reddish-brown coat

Black tail

COLOUR: BAY
Breed: Cleveland Bay

White mane

Gold coat

White tail

Sock marking

COLOUR: PALOMINO
Breed: Palomino

Black mane

Chestnut interspersed with white hairs

COLOUR: RED-ROAN
Breed: Ardennais

Black mane

Black coat

Black tail

COLOUR: BLACK
Breed: Friesian

White mane

White and black hairs on black skin

White tail

COLOUR: GREY
Breed: Camargue

Light brown mane

Spotted coat (here brown spots on white base)

Light brown tail

Sock marking

COLOUR: SPOTTED
Breed: Appaloosa

Black mane

Brown interspersed with black hairs

Brown tail

COLOUR: BROWN
Breed: Holstein

Reddish-gold mane

Reddish-gold tail

Sock marking

Reddish-gold coat

COLOUR: CHESTNUT
Breed: Frederiksborg

Skeleton

THE SKELETON IS A STRONG but flexible framework, made up of about 205 bones, that supports and protects the soft tissues of the body. The spinal vertebrae form a column that keeps the back rigid and strong enough to bear the weight of the body organs, and to transmit the propelling force of the hind limbs to the rest of the body. Joints, such as the hock and stifle, give the limbs flexibility and also act as shock absorbers. Each limb has only one digit (corresponding to the middle finger or toe of a human), which bears the horse's weight and is enclosed at the end by the hoof. In addition to supporting and protecting body organs, the skeleton has two other important functions. It acts as a store for the minerals calcium and phosphorus, and it helps to produce red and white blood corpuscles.

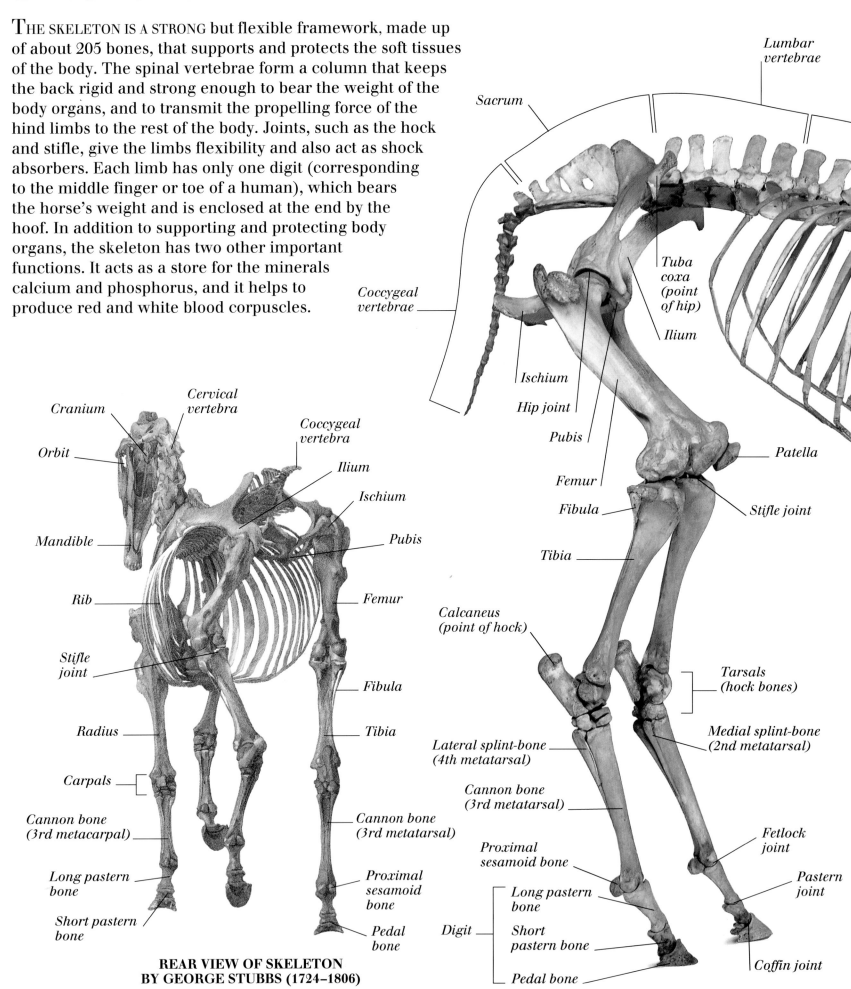

Lumbar vertebrae

Sacrum

Coccygeal vertebrae

Tuba coxa (point of hip)

Ilium

Ischium

Hip joint

Pubis

Femur

Fibula

Tibia

Patella

Stifle joint

Calcaneus (point of hock)

Tarsals (hock bones)

Lateral splint-bone (4th metatarsal)

Medial splint-bone (2nd metatarsal)

Cannon bone (3rd metatarsal)

Proximal sesamoid bone

Fetlock joint

Long pastern bone

Pastern joint

Digit

Short pastern bone

Pedal bone

Coffin joint

Cranium

Cervical vertebra

Coccygeal vertebra

Orbit

Ilium

Ischium

Mandible

Pubis

Rib

Femur

Stifle joint

Fibula

Radius

Tibia

Carpals

Cannon bone (3rd metatarsal)

Cannon bone (3rd metacarpal)

Long pastern bone

Proximal sesamoid bone

Short pastern bone

Pedal bone

**REAR VIEW OF SKELETON
BY GEORGE STUBBS (1724–1806)**

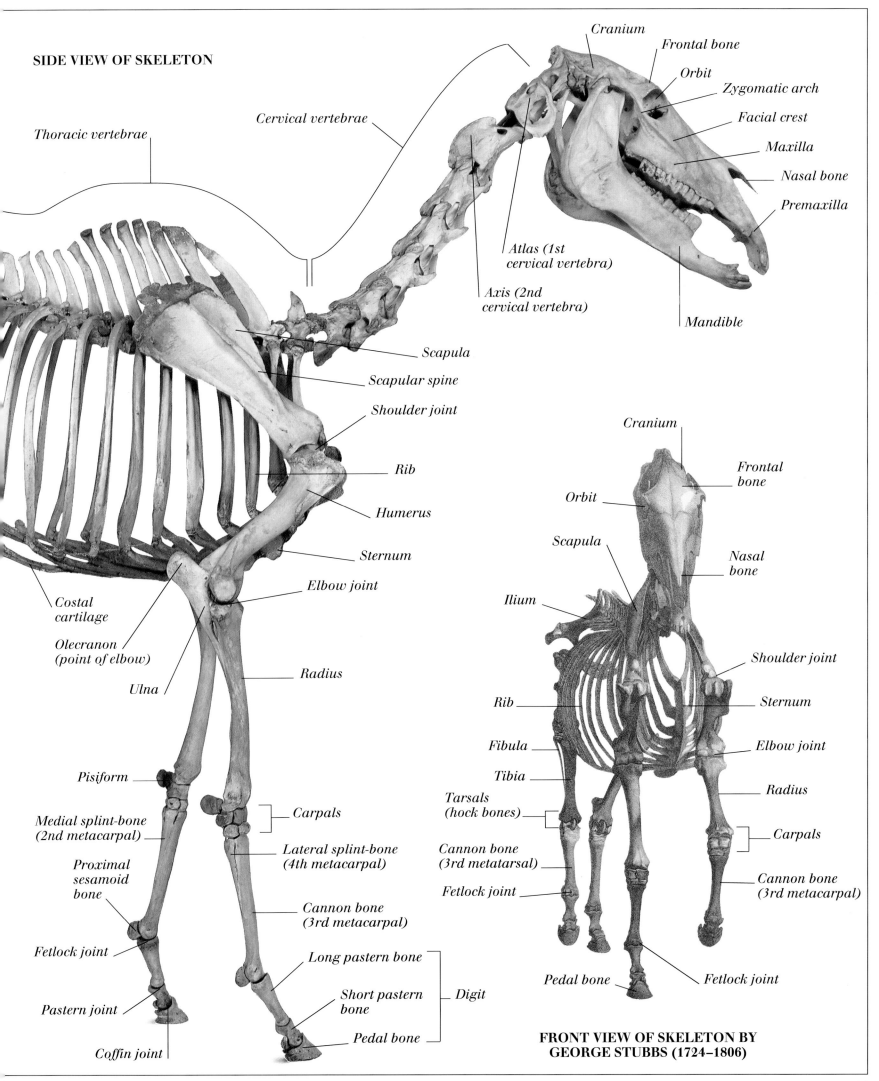

SIDE VIEW OF SKELETON

Cranium

Frontal bone

Orbit

Zygomatic arch

Facial crest

Maxilla

Nasal bone

Premaxilla

Cervical vertebrae

Thoracic vertebrae

Atlas (1st cervical vertebra)

Axis (2nd cervical vertebra)

Mandible

Scapula

Scapular spine

Shoulder joint

Rib

Humerus

Sternum

Elbow joint

Costal cartilage

Olecranon (point of elbow)

Ulna

Radius

Pisiform

Carpals

Medial splint-bone (2nd metacarpal)

Lateral splint-bone (4th metacarpal)

Proximal sesamoid bone

Cannon bone (3rd metacarpal)

Fetlock joint

Long pastern bone

Short pastern bone

Digit

Pastern joint

Pedal bone

Coffin joint

Cranium

Frontal bone

Orbit

Nasal bone

Scapula

Ilium

Shoulder joint

Rib

Sternum

Fibula

Elbow joint

Tibia

Radius

Tarsals (hock bones)

Carpals

Cannon bone (3rd metatarsal)

Cannon bone (3rd metacarpal)

Fetlock joint

Pedal bone

Fetlock joint

FRONT VIEW OF SKELETON BY GEORGE STUBBS (1724–1806)

11

Skull

**SKULL BY
GEORGE STUBBS
(1724–1806)**

THE SKULL IS MADE UP OF 34 bones (including the three small bones in each middle ear), most of which are fused together to form a strong, rigid structure that protects the brain and sensory organs of the head, and holds the teeth. At the back of the skull, two bones (called occipital condyles) make a flexible joint with the cervical vertebrae (neck bones). Above the occipital condyles is the cranium, which surrounds the cranial cavity that houses the brain. The brain is connected to the spinal cord through a passage called the foramen magnum. There are several other foramina (passages) to allow nerves and blood vessels to pass into and out of the skull. At the front of the skull are the large orbits that house the eyes, and the nasal bones that protect the nasal organs. Inside the skull there are spaces – called cavities if they contain organs, or sinuses if they contain only air. The largest bone of the skull is the mandible (lower jaw). Together with the maxilla and premaxilla (which form the upper jaw), the mandible holds the horse's teeth (see pp. 14-15).

SECTION THROUGH SKULL

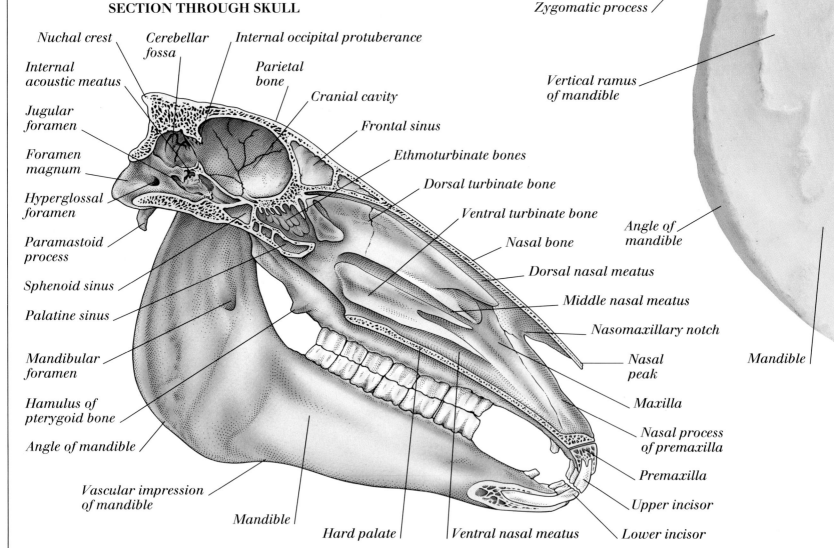

Nuchal crest

Parietal bone

Squamous part of temporal bone

Temporal crest

Occipital condyle

Paramastoid process

External auditory meatus

Condyle of mandible

Zygomatic process

Vertical ramus of mandible

Angle of mandible

Mandible

Cranium

Nuchal crest • Cerebellar fossa • Internal occipital protuberance

Internal acoustic meatus

Parietal bone

Jugular foramen

Cranial cavity

Foramen magnum

Frontal sinus

Ethmoturbinate bones

Hyperglossal foramen

Dorsal turbinate bone

Ventral turbinate bone

Paramastoid process

Nasal bone

Sphenoid sinus

Dorsal nasal meatus

Palatine sinus

Middle nasal meatus

Nasomaxillary notch

Mandibular foramen

Nasal peak

Hamulus of pterygoid bone

Maxilla

Angle of mandible

Nasal process of premaxilla

Premaxilla

Vascular impression of mandible

Upper incisor

Mandible | Hard palate | Ventral nasal meatus | Lower incisor

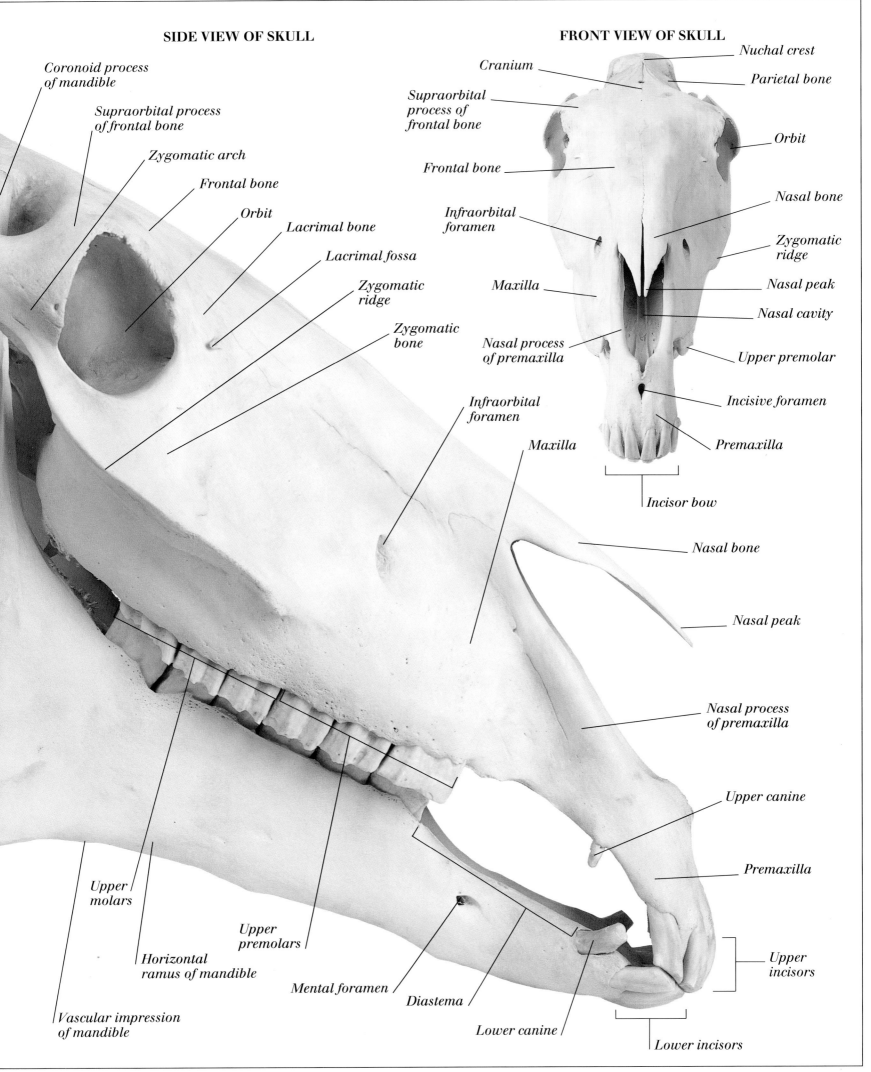

SIDE VIEW OF SKULL

Coronoid process
of mandible

Supraorbital process
of frontal bone

Zygomatic arch

Frontal bone

Orbit

Lacrimal bone

Lacrimal fossa

Zygomatic
ridge

Zygomatic
bone

Infraorbital
foramen

Maxilla

Upper
molars

Horizontal
ramus of mandible

Upper
premolars

Mental foramen

Diastema

Lower canine

Vascular impression
of mandible

FRONT VIEW OF SKULL

Cranium

Nuchal crest

Parietal bone

Supraorbital
process of
frontal bone

Orbit

Frontal bone

Nasal bone

Infraorbital
foramen

Zygomatic
ridge

Maxilla

Nasal peak

Nasal cavity

Nasal process
of premaxilla

Upper premolar

Incisive foramen

Premaxilla

Incisor bow

Nasal bone

Nasal peak

Nasal process
of premaxilla

Upper canine

Premaxilla

Upper
incisors

Lower incisors

13

Teeth

STRONG TEETH AND JAWS enable the horse to eat its staple food of grass. The high-crowned teeth are held in the powerful bone structures of the premaxilla and maxilla (which together form the upper jaw) and the mandible (lower jaw). The foal has a set of milk teeth that wear down as it begins to graze. Then the adult or permanent teeth gradually replace the milk teeth, so that the horse has a complete set of permanent teeth by the time it is five years old. An adult horse usually has 40 teeth – 12 incisors, 4 canines, 12 premolars, and 12 molars – although in the female the canines may be small or absent. Permanent teeth have short roots and long crowns when they first erupt, but the crowns wear down as the horse ages. Teeth are composed of vertical layers of enamel, dentine, and cement that wear down at different rates, leaving the surface uneven and exposing different surface features. The age of a horse can be estimated from the wear on its teeth, particularly on the surface of the incisors, and from the development of Galvayne's groove.

DEVELOPMENT OF GALVAYNE'S GROOVE

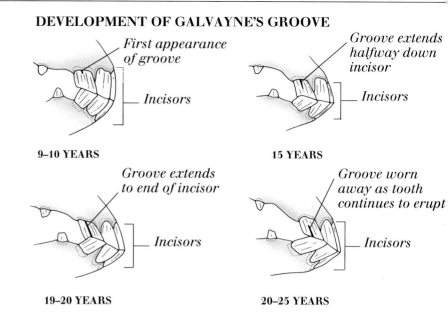

First appearance of groove

Incisors

9–10 YEARS

Groove extends halfway down incisor

Incisors

15 YEARS

Groove extends to end of incisor

Incisors

19–20 YEARS

Groove worn away as tooth continues to erupt

Incisors

20–25 YEARS

EROSION OF CENTRAL INCISOR

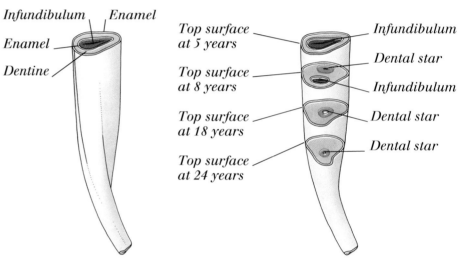

Infundibulum *Enamel*

Enamel

Dentine

Top surface at 5 years

Top surface at 8 years

Top surface at 18 years

Top surface at 24 years

Infundibulum

Dental star

Infundibulum

Dental star

Dental star

INCISOR AT 5 YEARS

STAGES OF EROSION

DEVELOPMENT OF TEETH

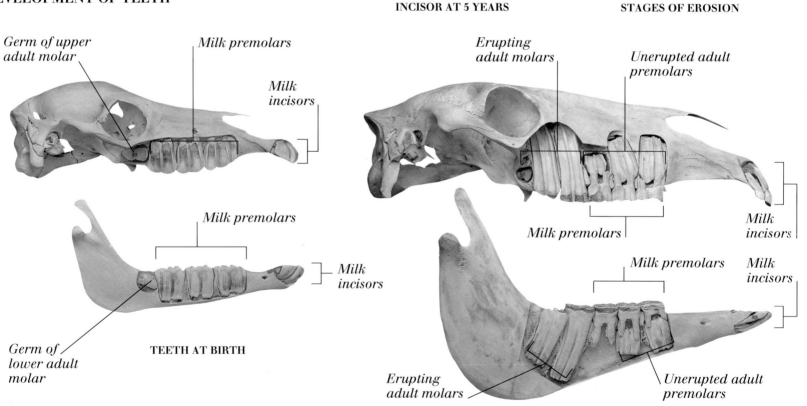

Germ of upper adult molar

Milk premolars

Milk incisors

Milk premolars

Milk incisors

Germ of lower adult molar

TEETH AT BIRTH

Erupting adult molars

Unerupted adult premolars

Milk premolars

Milk incisors

Milk premolars

Milk incisors

Erupting adult molars

Unerupted adult premolars

TEETH AT 2 YEARS

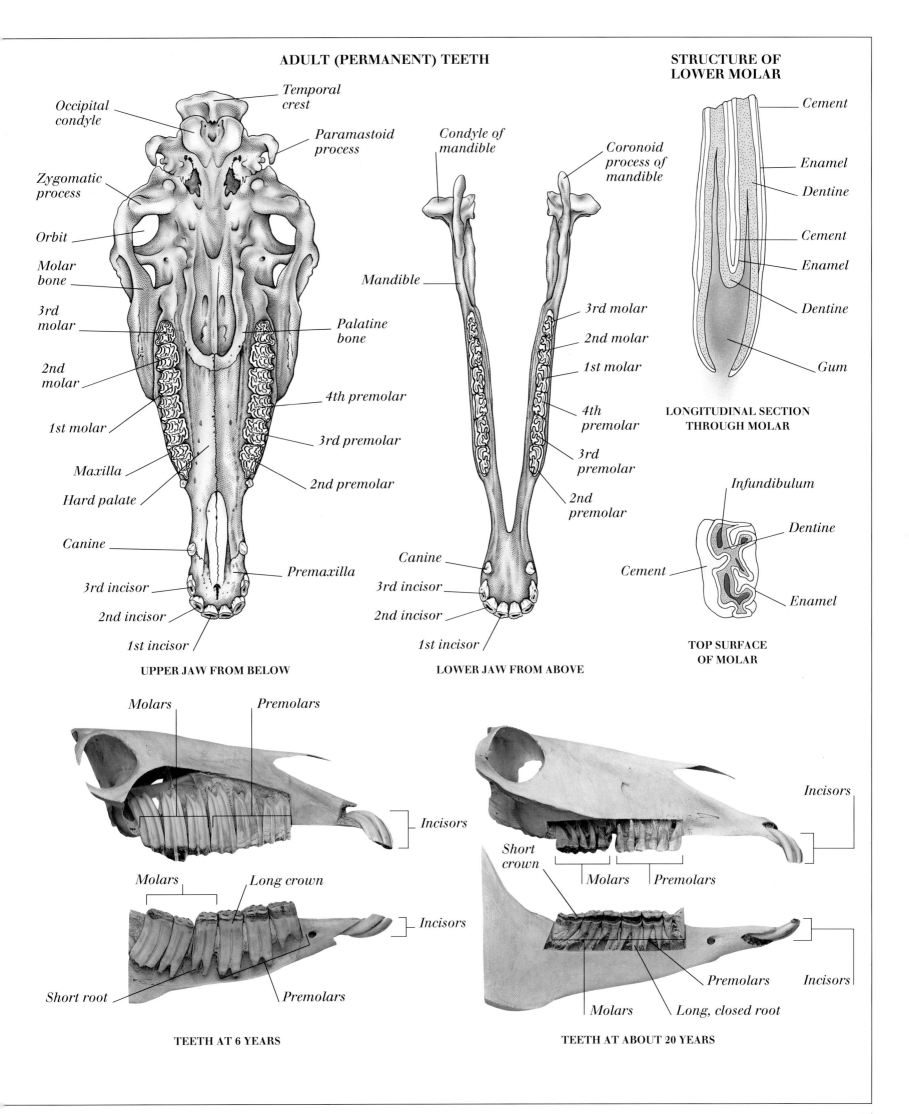

ADULT (PERMANENT) TEETH

UPPER JAW FROM BELOW

Occipital condyle

Temporal crest

Paramastoid process

Zygomatic process

Orbit

Molar bone

3rd molar

2nd molar

1st molar

Maxilla

Hard palate

Canine

3rd incisor

2nd incisor

1st incisor

Palatine bone

4th premolar

3rd premolar

2nd premolar

Premaxilla

LOWER JAW FROM ABOVE

Condyle of mandible

Coronoid process of mandible

Mandible

3rd molar

2nd molar

1st molar

4th premolar

3rd premolar

2nd premolar

Canine

3rd incisor

2nd incisor

1st incisor

STRUCTURE OF LOWER MOLAR

Cement

Enamel

Dentine

Cement

Enamel

Dentine

Gum

LONGITUDINAL SECTION THROUGH MOLAR

Infundibulum

Dentine

Cement

Enamel

TOP SURFACE OF MOLAR

Molars

Premolars

Incisors

Molars

Long crown

Incisors

Short root

Premolars

TEETH AT 6 YEARS

Short crown

Incisors

Molars

Premolars

Premolars

Incisors

Molars

Long, closed root

TEETH AT ABOUT 20 YEARS

Muscles

THE HORSE'S STAMINA, STRENGTH, AND AGILITY are largely due to a well-developed muscle system and a strong skeleton (see pp. 10-11). Muscle consists of fibrous bands of tissue that can contract and relax to produce movement. The horse has muscles in every part of its body, from inside the eye to the wall of the intestine, and from the heart to the limbs. There are two main types of muscles: voluntary and involuntary. Voluntary muscles are consciously controlled by the horse and are responsible for movements such as walking, galloping, and chewing. In contrast, involuntary muscles contract and relax without the horse's conscious control. The heart is made up of a special type of muscle, known as cardiac muscle. Involuntary muscles are responsible for automatic actions, such as changing the size of the pupil in the eye and moving food along the intestine. Most voluntary muscles are large, superficial muscles that lie immediately beneath the skin; these are the muscles shown in the illustrations here. Most involuntary muscles form an integral part of certain organs, such as the stomach. The superficial muscles are attached to the skeleton by cords of dense tissue called tendons, and the bones are connected together by bands of tough fibrous tissue called ligaments.

External abdominal oblique muscle

Gluteal fascia

Tensor fascial latae muscle

Coccygeus muscle

Superficial gluteal muscle

Semitendinosus muscle

Tail depressor muscles

Biceps femoris muscle

Deep digital flexor muscle

Lateral digital extensor muscle

Aponeurosis of external abdominal oblique muscle

Lateral femoral fascia

Popliteus muscle

Cranial tibial muscle

Long digital extensor muscle

Lateral digital extensor tendon

Deep digital flexor tendon

Suspensory ligament

Superficial digital flexor tendon

Suspensory ligament

Lateral digital extensor muscle

Splenius muscle

Masseter muscle

Semitendinosus muscle

Semimembranosus muscle

Biceps femoris muscle

Triceps muscle

Lateral carpal flexor muscle

Deep digital flexor muscle

Gracilis muscle

Lateral digital extensor muscle

Superficial digital flexor tendon

Superficial digital flexor tendon

REAR VIEW OF MUSCLES BY GEORGE STUBBS (1724–1806)

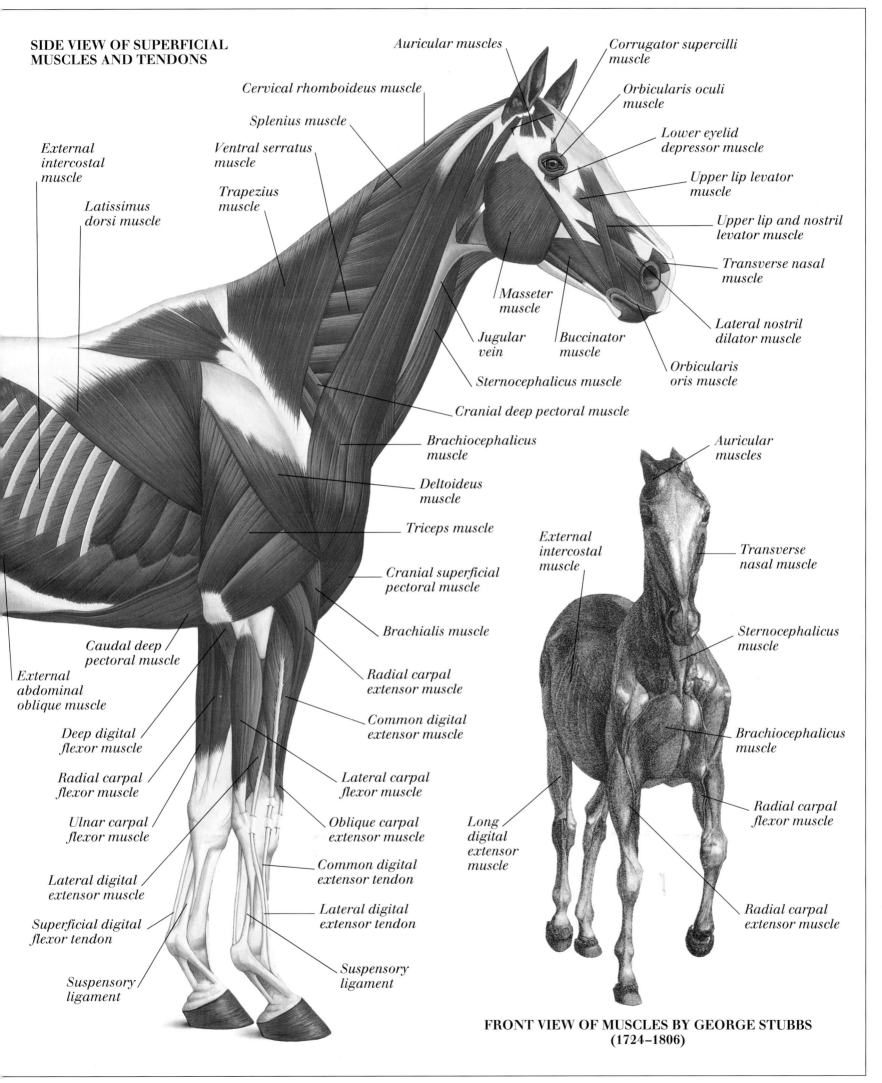

SIDE VIEW OF SUPERFICIAL MUSCLES AND TENDONS

Auricular muscles

Corrugator supercilli muscle

Cervical rhomboideus muscle

Orbicularis oculi muscle

Splenius muscle

Lower eyelid depressor muscle

External intercostal muscle

Ventral serratus muscle

Upper lip levator muscle

Trapezius muscle

Latissimus dorsi muscle

Upper lip and nostril levator muscle

Transverse nasal muscle

Masseter muscle

Lateral nostril dilator muscle

Jugular vein

Buccinator muscle

Sternocephalicus muscle

Orbicularis oris muscle

Cranial deep pectoral muscle

Brachiocephalicus muscle

Auricular muscles

Deltoideus muscle

External intercostal muscle

Transverse nasal muscle

Triceps muscle

Cranial superficial pectoral muscle

Sternocephalicus muscle

Brachialis muscle

Caudal deep pectoral muscle

Radial carpal extensor muscle

Brachiocephalicus muscle

External abdominal oblique muscle

Common digital extensor muscle

Deep digital flexor muscle

Lateral carpal flexor muscle

Radial carpal extensor muscle

Radial carpal flexor muscle

Ulnar carpal flexor muscle

Oblique carpal extensor muscle

Long digital extensor muscle

Lateral digital extensor muscle

Common digital extensor tendon

Lateral digital extensor tendon

Radial carpal extensor muscle

Superficial digital flexor tendon

Suspensory ligament

Suspensory ligament

FRONT VIEW OF MUSCLES BY GEORGE STUBBS (1724–1806)

17

Nervous system

THE NERVOUS SYSTEM is a complex information processing and storage network that enables the horse to detect and react to changes inside and outside its body; to automatically control various internal processes, such as the beating of the heart; and to initiate conscious actions, such as walking. It consists of two parts: the central nervous system, comprising the brain and spinal cord; and the peripheral nervous system, comprising sensory organs, such as the eyes and ears, and the network of nerves that connects the brain and spinal cord to the rest of the body. The brain has three main regions: the brainstem, cerebellum, and cerebrum. The brainstem performs many functions, including relaying information from the spinal cord and regulating respiration and blood circulation. The cerebellum controls balance and the coordination of voluntary muscles. The cerebrum processes information from the sensory organs, and is also responsible for many conscious and intelligent activities. The main function of the spinal cord is to carry messages to and from the brain, and to mediate certain reflex actions. The peripheral nervous system carries messages from sensory organs to the central nervous system, and transmits messages from the central nervous system to muscles, organs, and glands throughout the body.

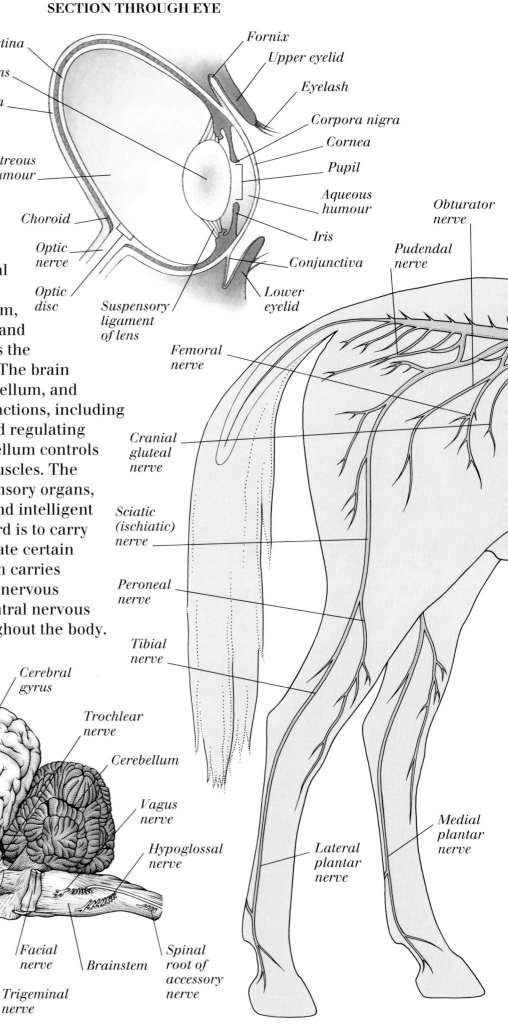

SECTION THROUGH EYE

Retina
Lens
Sclera
Vitreous humour
Choroid
Optic nerve
Optic disc
Suspensory ligament of lens
Fornix
Upper eyelid
Eyelash
Corpora nigra
Cornea
Pupil
Aqueous humour
Iris
Conjunctiva
Lower eyelid

Obturator nerve
Pudendal nerve
Cranial gluteal nerve
Sciatic (ischiatic) nerve
Peroneal nerve
Tibial nerve
Femoral nerve
Lateral plantar nerve
Medial plantar nerve

SIDE VIEW OF BRAIN

Cerebral sulcus
Cerebral gyrus
Cerebrum
Trochlear nerve
Cerebellum
Vagus nerve
Hypoglossal nerve
Spinal root of accessory nerve
Brainstem
Facial nerve
Trigeminal nerve
Cerebral crus
Oculomotor nerve
Pituitary
Optic tract
Olfactory bulb

SIDE VIEW OF NERVOUS SYSTEM

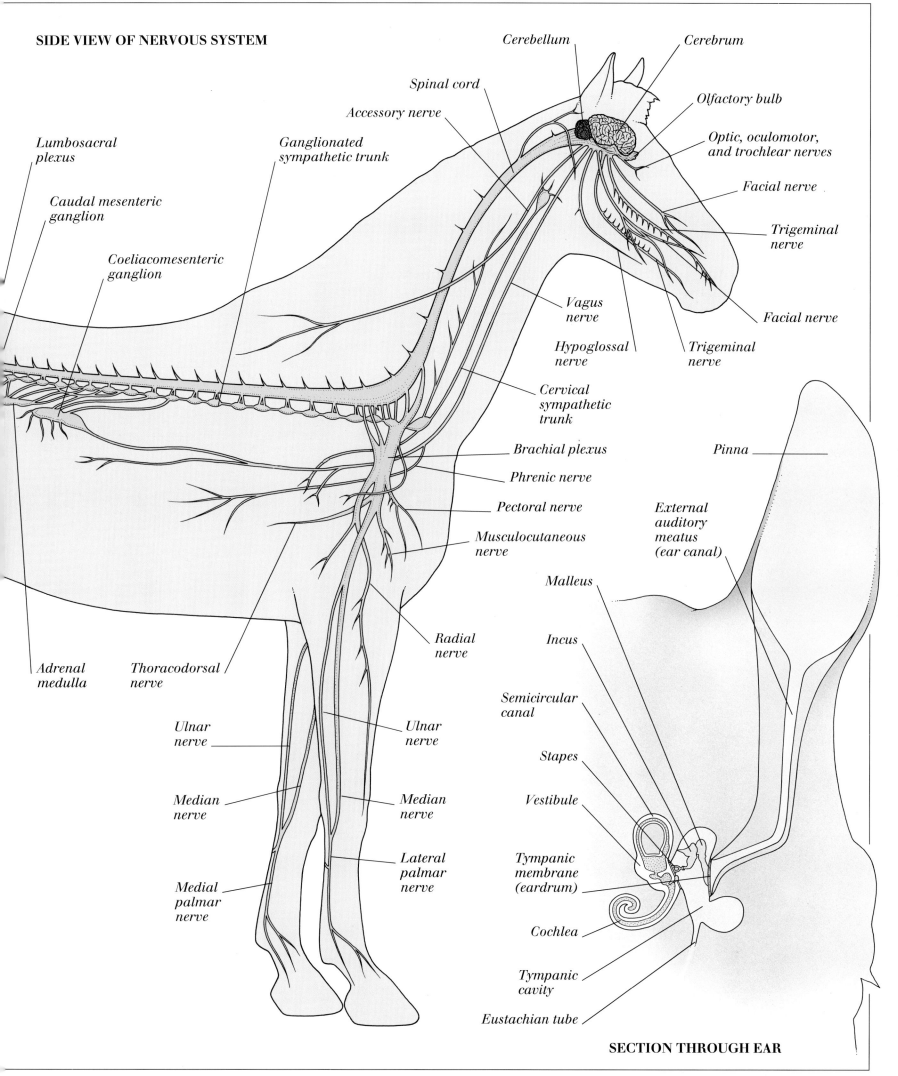

Cerebellum

Cerebrum

Spinal cord

Olfactory bulb

Accessory nerve

Optic, oculomotor, and trochlear nerves

Ganglionated sympathetic trunk

Facial nerve

Lumbosacral plexus

Trigeminal nerve

Caudal mesenteric ganglion

Vagus nerve

Facial nerve

Coeliacomesenteric ganglion

Hypoglossal nerve

Trigeminal nerve

Cervical sympathetic trunk

Brachial plexus

Pinna

Phrenic nerve

Pectoral nerve

External auditory meatus (ear canal)

Musculocutaneous nerve

Malleus

Radial nerve

Incus

Semicircular canal

Adrenal medulla

Thoracodorsal nerve

Stapes

Ulnar nerve

Ulnar nerve

Vestibule

Median nerve

Median nerve

Tympanic membrane (eardrum)

Lateral palmar nerve

Medial palmar nerve

Cochlea

Tympanic cavity

Eustachian tube

SECTION THROUGH EAR

19

Respiratory and circulatory systems

THE RESPIRATORY AND CIRCULATORY systems together supply oxygen to, and remove carbon dioxide from, every cell in the horse's body. The circulatory system also carries nutrients and other substances around the body in the blood. The respiratory system consists of the air passages (nasal passages and trachea) and lungs. Air is inhaled into the lungs, and oxygen in the air passes across the thin lung walls and into the blood. Meanwhile, carbon dioxide passes out of the blood into the lungs and is breathed out of the body during exhalation. The circulatory system consists of the heart and blood vessels (arteries, veins, and capillaries). The heart pumps deoxygenated blood (shown in blue in the illustrations) to the lungs, where it becomes oxygenated (shown in red) and returns to the heart. The oxygenated blood is then pumped through arteries to the rest of the body. The blood passes from the arteries into the capillaries, where the body cells take up the oxygen and release carbon dioxide and other waste products into the blood. The blood (now deoxygenated) returns through the veins to the heart, and the cycle continues.

SECTION THROUGH LUNGS

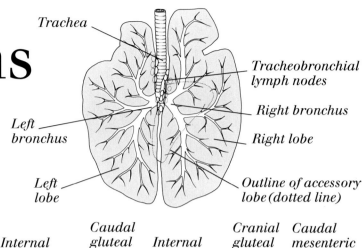

Trachea

Tracheobronchial lymph nodes

Left bronchus

Right bronchus

Right lobe

Left lobe

Outline of accessory lobe (dotted line)

SECTION THROUGH HEART

Cranial vena cava

Aorta

Pectinate muscles

Pulmonary trunk

Right atrium

Aortic valve

Right coronary artery

Pulmonary vein

Right atrioventricular valve

Left atrium

Chordae tendineae

Great cardiac vein

Septomarginal trabecula

Left coronary artery

Right ventricle

Left atrioventricular valve

Ventricular septum

Chordae tendineae

Left ventricle

Papillary muscle

Septomarginal trabecula

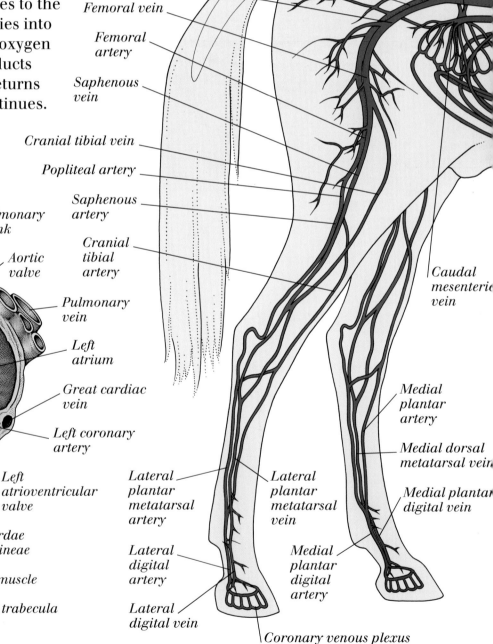

Caudal gluteal artery

Cranial gluteal artery

Caudal mesenteric artery

Internal iliac artery

Internal iliac vein

External iliac artery

External iliac vein

Femoral vein

Femoral artery

Saphenous vein

Cranial tibial vein

Popliteal artery

Saphenous artery

Cranial tibial artery

Caudal mesenteric vein

Medial plantar artery

Medial dorsal metatarsal vein

Lateral plantar metatarsal artery

Lateral plantar metatarsal vein

Medial plantar digital vein

Lateral digital artery

Medial plantar digital artery

Lateral digital vein

Coronary venous plexus

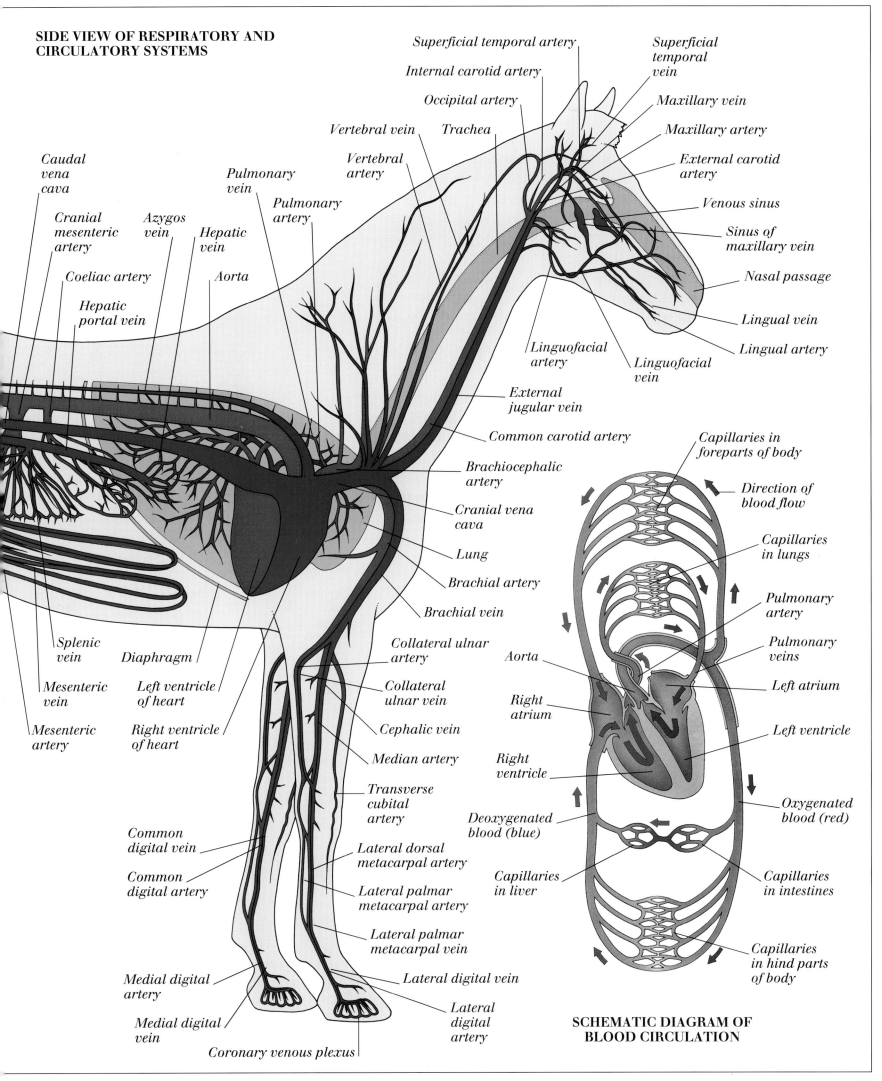

SIDE VIEW OF RESPIRATORY AND CIRCULATORY SYSTEMS

Superficial temporal artery

Internal carotid artery

Occipital artery

Superficial temporal vein

Maxillary vein

Maxillary artery

Vertebral vein

Trachea

External carotid artery

Vertebral artery

Venous sinus

Pulmonary vein

Sinus of maxillary vein

Caudal vena cava

Pulmonary artery

Nasal passage

Cranial mesenteric artery

Azygos vein

Hepatic vein

Lingual vein

Coeliac artery

Aorta

Lingual artery

Hepatic portal vein

Linguofacial artery

Linguofacial vein

External jugular vein

Common carotid artery

Brachiocephalic artery

Cranial vena cava

Lung

Brachial artery

Brachial vein

Splenic vein

Collateral ulnar artery

Diaphragm

Collateral ulnar vein

Mesenteric vein

Left ventricle of heart

Cephalic vein

Mesenteric artery

Right ventricle of heart

Median artery

Transverse cubital artery

Common digital vein

Lateral dorsal metacarpal artery

Common digital artery

Lateral palmar metacarpal artery

Lateral palmar metacarpal vein

Medial digital artery

Lateral digital vein

Medial digital vein

Lateral digital artery

Coronary venous plexus

Capillaries in foreparts of body

Direction of blood flow

Capillaries in lungs

Pulmonary artery

Pulmonary veins

Aorta

Left atrium

Right atrium

Left ventricle

Right ventricle

Deoxygenated blood (blue)

Oxygenated blood (red)

Capillaries in liver

Capillaries in intestines

Capillaries in hind parts of body

SCHEMATIC DIAGRAM OF BLOOD CIRCULATION

Digestive system

THE DIGESTIVE SYSTEM breaks down food by chemical and physical processes so that it can be absorbed by the body tissues and used to provide raw materials for energy, growth, and cell maintenance. The system consists of the alimentary tract (which extends from the mouth to the anus) and associated organs and glands that secrete digestive juices. Digestion begins in the mouth, where grass (the staple food of horses) is physically ground down by chewing and chemically broken down by saliva. Physical breakdown continues as food is churned and pushed along the alimentary tract by muscular contractions of the tract wall. Chemical breakdown also continues as food is digested by gastric juices in the stomach and by enzymes in the small intestine. Further breakdown occurs in the caecum and colon, where microorganisms produce enzymes that break down cellulose (a major constituent of grass). The products of digestion are absorbed into the blood mainly from the small intestine and caecum, although fluids are absorbed chiefly from the colon. Indigestible food is stored in the rectum until it is expelled through the anus as faeces.

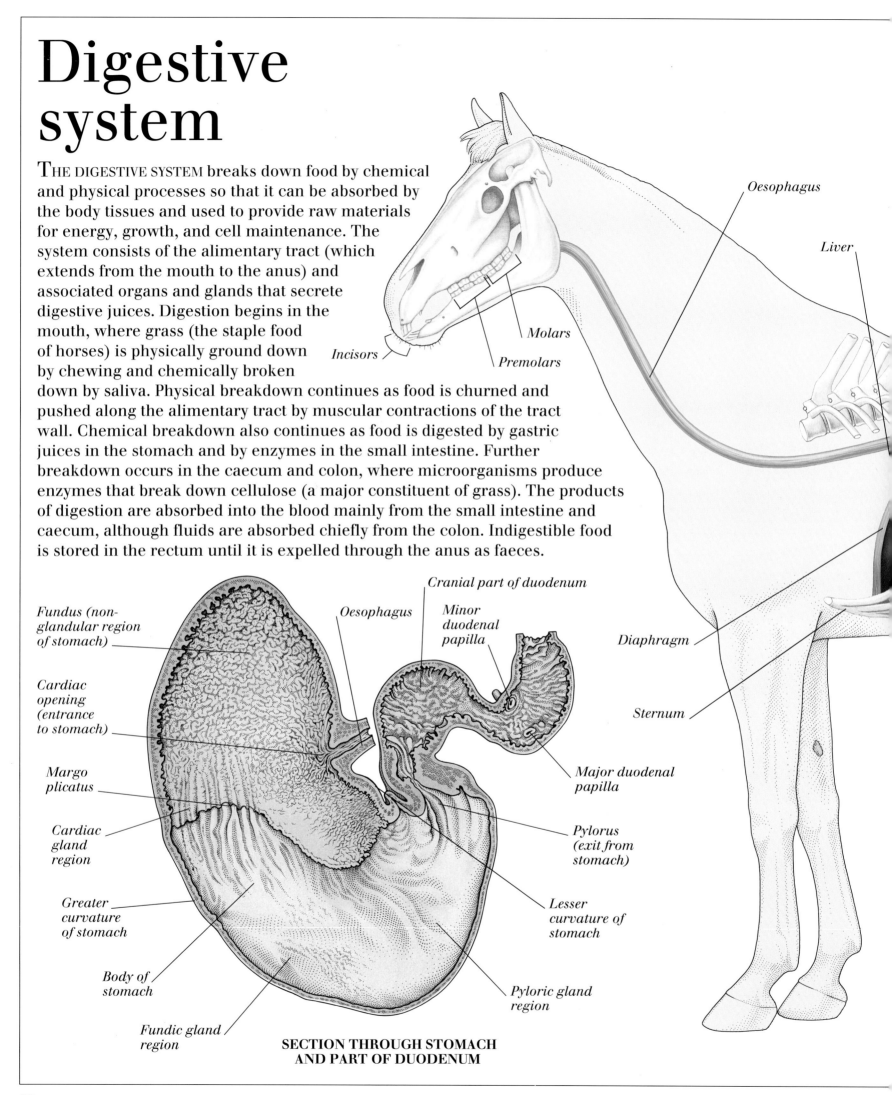

Oesophagus

Liver

Molars

Incisors

Premolars

Diaphragm

Sternum

Fundus (non-glandular region of stomach)

Cardiac opening (entrance to stomach)

Margo plicatus

Cardiac gland region

Greater curvature of stomach

Body of stomach

Fundic gland region

Oesophagus

Cranial part of duodenum

Minor duodenal papilla

Major duodenal papilla

Pylorus (exit from stomach)

Lesser curvature of stomach

Pyloric gland region

SECTION THROUGH STOMACH AND PART OF DUODENUM

SIDE VIEW OF DIGESTIVE SYSTEM

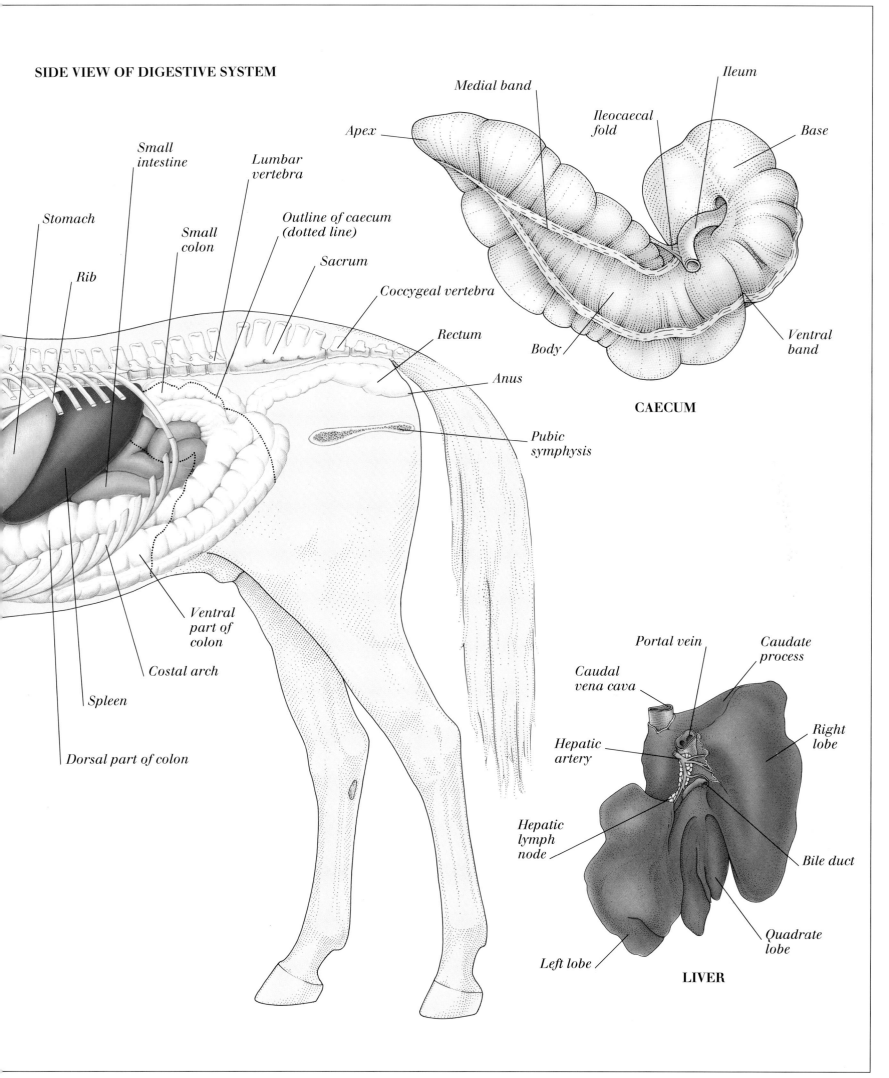

Small intestine

Stomach

Rib

Small colon

Lumbar vertebra

Outline of caecum (dotted line)

Sacrum

Coccygeal vertebra

Rectum

Anus

Pubic symphysis

Ventral part of colon

Costal arch

Spleen

Dorsal part of colon

Medial band

Apex

Ileocaecal fold

Ileum

Base

Ventral band

Body

CAECUM

Portal vein

Caudate process

Caudal vena cava

Hepatic artery

Right lobe

Hepatic lymph node

Bile duct

Left lobe

Quadrate lobe

LIVER

Urinogenital system

THE URINARY AND REPRODUCTIVE ORGANS (which together make up the urinogenital system) are situated close together in the lower abdominal and pelvic region. The urinary system regulates the body's water balance and removes waste products. It consists of the kidneys, ureters, bladder, and urethra. The kidneys filter waste products, salts, and water from the blood to produce urine. The urine passes through the ureters to the bladder and then out of the body through the urethra. The reproductive organs produce sex cells: sperm in the male and ova (eggs) in the female. The other main function of the female reproductive system is to nurture a fetus. A male horse typically reaches sexual maturity at about 18 months old, after which its testes begin to produce sperm. The sperm pass from the testes to the epididymides, where they mature. During copulation, the sperm pass down the urethra and out of the erect penis. A female horse typically reaches sexual maturity between the ages of one and three years, after which the ovaries begin to produce ova. When a mature mare is in season (periodically between spring and autumn), the ova pass through the fallopian tubes to the uterus. If the mare is mated, an ovum may be fertilized by a sperm to produce a fetus (see pp. 26-27).

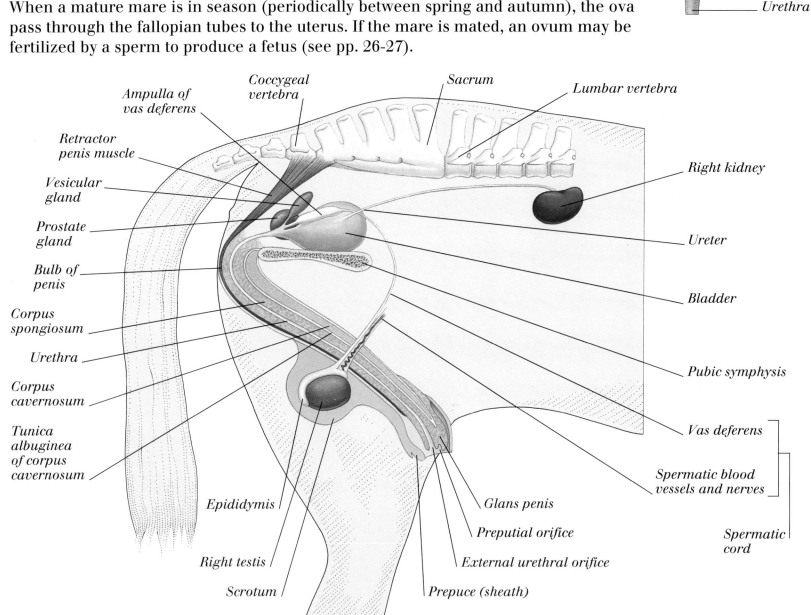

Left kidney
Right kidney
Renal artery
Renal vein
Aorta
Vena cava
Left ureter
Right ureter
Bladder
Urethra

Ampulla of vas deferens
Coccygeal vertebra
Sacrum
Lumbar vertebra
Retractor penis muscle
Vesicular gland
Prostate gland
Bulb of penis
Corpus spongiosum
Urethra
Corpus cavernosum
Tunica albuginea of corpus cavernosum
Right kidney
Ureter
Bladder
Pubic symphysis
Vas deferens
Spermatic blood vessels and nerves
Spermatic cord
Epididymis
Glans penis
Preputial orifice
Right testis
External urethral orifice
Scrotum
Prepuce (sheath)

SIDE VIEW OF MALE URINOGENITAL SYSTEM

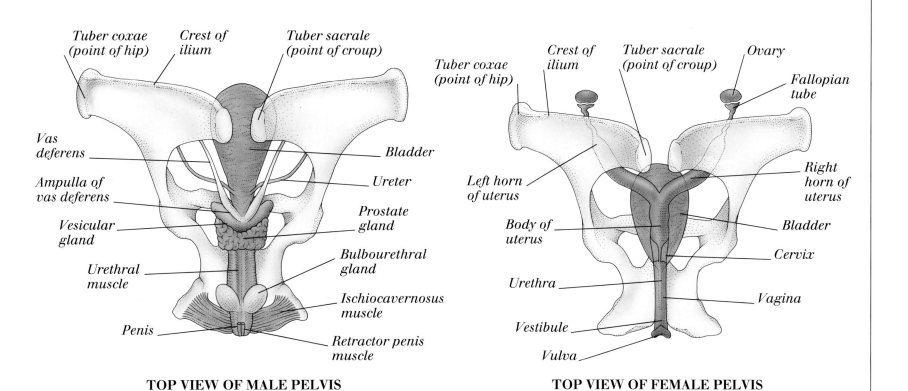

TOP VIEW OF MALE PELVIS

Tuber coxae (point of hip)
Crest of ilium
Tuber sacrale (point of croup)
Vas deferens
Ampulla of vas deferens
Vesicular gland
Urethral muscle
Penis
Bladder
Ureter
Prostate gland
Bulbourethral gland
Ischiocavernosus muscle
Retractor penis muscle

TOP VIEW OF FEMALE PELVIS

Crest of ilium
Tuber sacrale (point of croup)
Ovary
Fallopian tube
Tuber coxae (point of hip)
Left horn of uterus
Right horn of uterus
Body of uterus
Bladder
Cervix
Urethra
Vagina
Vestibule
Vulva

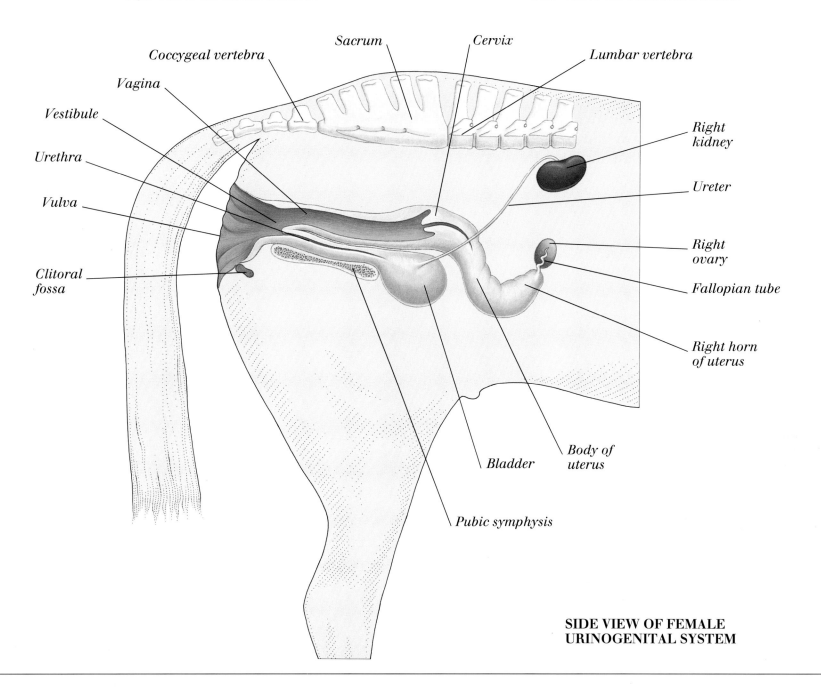

Sacrum
Cervix
Coccygeal vertebra
Lumbar vertebra
Vagina
Vestibule
Urethra
Right kidney
Ureter
Vulva
Right ovary
Clitoral fossa
Fallopian tube
Right horn of uterus
Body of uterus
Bladder
Pubic symphysis

SIDE VIEW OF FEMALE URINOGENITAL SYSTEM

Development and growth

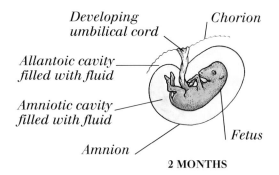

Developing umbilical cord — *Chorion*

Allantoic cavity filled with fluid

Amniotic cavity filled with fluid

Amnion

Fetus

2 MONTHS

TEN-YEAR-OLD SHIRE MARE AND HER FIVE-WEEK-OLD FOAL

MARES THAT ARE SEXUALLY MATURE come into season (also known as oestrus) every year between spring and autumn. When in season, it is possible for a mare to mate and to conceive a foal (it is rare for a mare to have twins). The fetus takes about 11 months to develop in the mare's uterus; this is known as the gestation period. At the end of the gestation period, the foal is ready to be born. The mare usually lies down to give birth. When the foal is being born, its front feet normally emerge first, followed by its head and then the rest of its body. Immediately after the birth, the mare gets up and licks her newborn foal clean, which also helps the foal's circulation and breathing. Within about an hour of being born, the foal is able to stand up, and it begins to suck milk from its mother's teats. The foal lives on its mother's milk alone for the first two months and then gradually begins to eat grass until it is fully weaned at about six months old. Foals and young horses – known as fillies if they are female, or colts if they are male – grow relatively quickly. They reach adult size between the age of four and five years, by which time they also have their full set of adult teeth (see pp. 14-15).

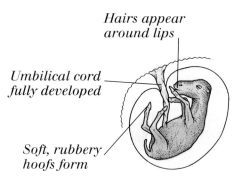

Hairs appear around lips

Umbilical cord fully developed

Soft, rubbery hoofs form

4 MONTHS

DEVELOPMENT OF A FOAL

Large cranium

Eyes open from birth

Short face

Short, small body

Wide-based stance for stability

Small mouth

Long, thin limbs

Small, soft hoofs

NEWBORN FOAL

Upright, feathery mane

Large eyes

Large nostrils

FOAL AT 2 WEEKS

Soft, woolly coat, known as milk hair

Croup higher than withers

Cannon bone becomes longer

Upright stance

FOAL AT 5 WEEKS

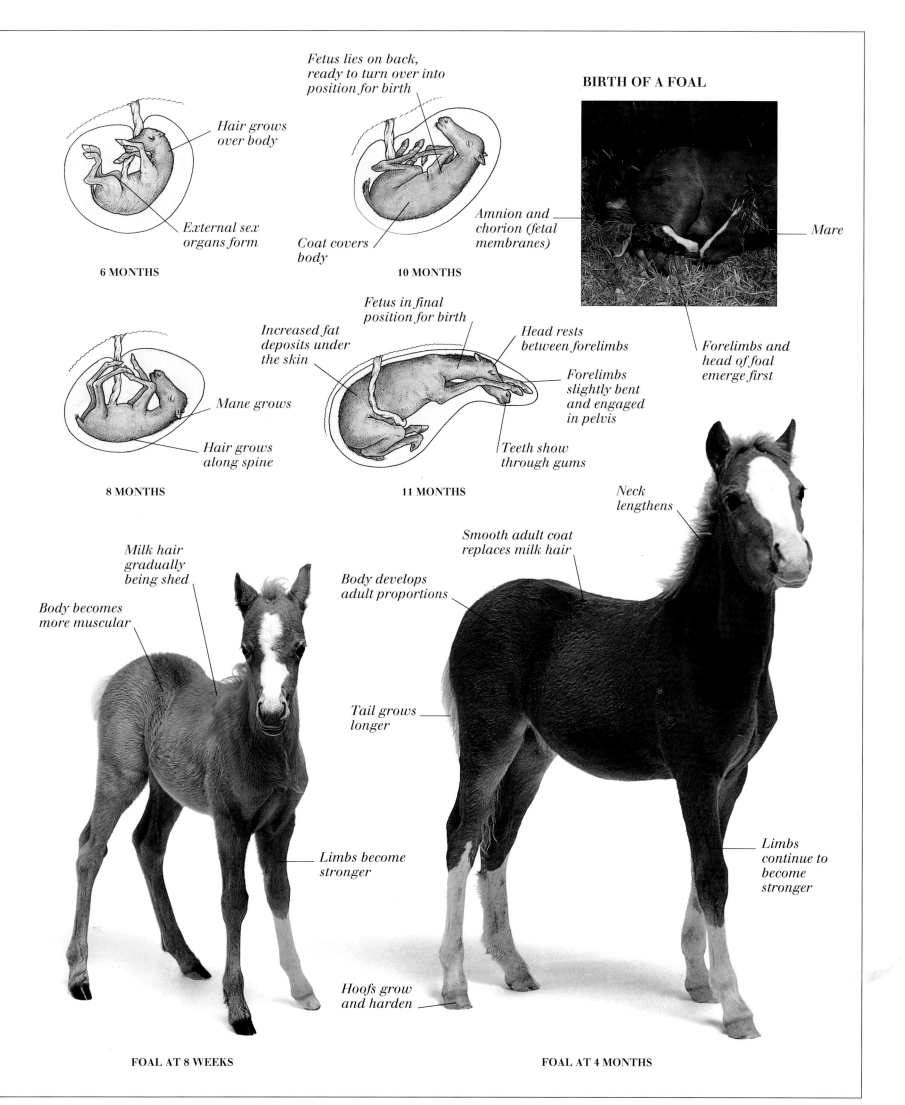

Hair grows over body

External sex organs form

6 MONTHS

Fetus lies on back, ready to turn over into position for birth

Amnion and chorion (fetal membranes)

Coat covers body

10 MONTHS

Increased fat deposits under the skin

Mane grows

Hair grows along spine

8 MONTHS

Fetus in final position for birth

Head rests between forelimbs

Forelimbs slightly bent and engaged in pelvis

Teeth show through gums

11 MONTHS

BIRTH OF A FOAL

Mare

Forelimbs and head of foal emerge first

Neck lengthens

Smooth adult coat replaces milk hair

Body develops adult proportions

Tail grows longer

Milk hair gradually being shed

Body becomes more muscular

Limbs become stronger

Hoofs grow and harden

Limbs continue to become stronger

FOAL AT 8 WEEKS

FOAL AT 4 MONTHS

Ponies 1

A PONY CAN BE DEFINED AS ANY HORSE that is 14.2 hands (147 cm) or less in height. Typical characteristics of ponies are deep, compact bodies; great strength in relation to their height; long, thick manes and tails; good endurance; and a natural hardiness that enables them to thrive in harsh environments. Some breeds – the Falabella, for example – have horse-like characteristics and are therefore sometimes considered to be horses rather than ponies despite their small size. There are many breeds of ponies, and their features vary depending on the conditions in the region where they evolved. Ponies whose natural habitats are the inhospitable terrain and cold climates of northern Europe and Asia – the Dartmoor pony, for example – tend to be small and stocky with thick coats. In contrast, ponies such as the Caspian (see pp. 30-31) that originate from the warmer climates of the Middle East and Africa tend to have longer, lighter bodies and thinner coats. Most ponies are easy to train, and are put to a wide variety of uses. For example, the New Forest and Australian ponies are suitable for riding. Other ponies, such as the Fjord, can also be used as pack animals, or for agricultural and light harness work.

FALABELLA

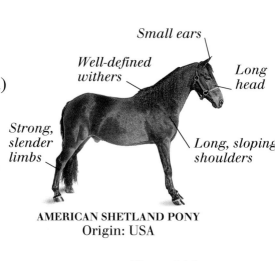

Small ears
Well-defined withers
Long head
Strong, slender limbs
Long, sloping shoulders

AMERICAN SHETLAND PONY
Origin: USA

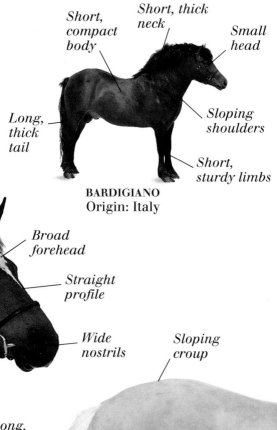

Short, compact body
Short, thick neck
Small head
Long, thick tail
Sloping shoulders
Short, sturdy limbs

BARDIGIANO
Origin: Italy

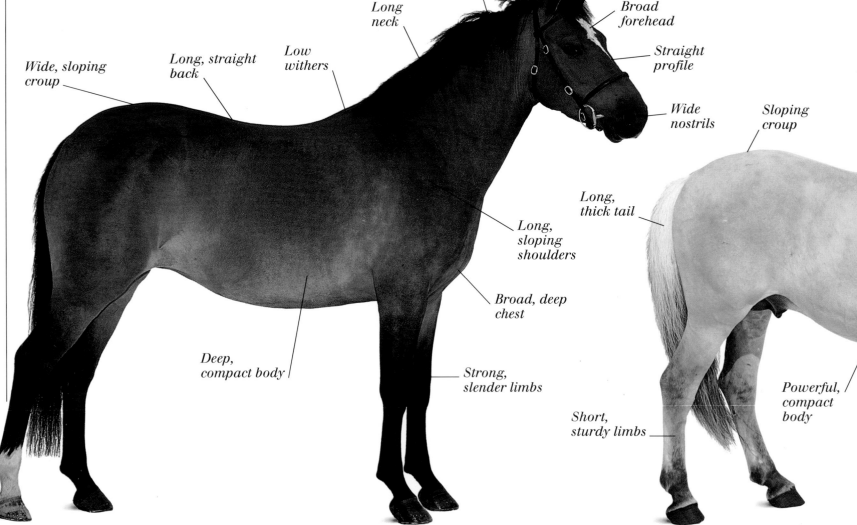

Thick mane
Long neck
Low withers
Long, straight back
Wide, sloping croup
Broad forehead
Straight profile
Wide nostrils
Sloping croup
Long, thick tail
Long, sloping shoulders
Broad, deep chest
Deep, compact body
Strong, slender limbs
Powerful, compact body
Short, sturdy limbs

NEW FOREST PONY
Origin: England

FJORD PONY
Origin: Norway

ROCKY MOUNTAIN PONY
Origin: USA

Long neck
Low withers
Long, flaxen tail
Long, flaxen mane
Strong, slender limbs

WELSH PONY
Origin: Wales

Small ears
Long neck
Powerful hindquarters
Sloping shoulders
Strong, slender limbs

HIGHLAND PONY
Origin: Scotland

Long neck
Small ears
Dorsal stripe
Sloping croup
Deep, compact body
Short cannon bone
Feather on limbs

BASHKIR
Origin: Russian Federation

Long mane
Low withers
Short, flat back
Short, thick neck
Sloping shoulders
Short cannon bone
Short, sturdy limbs

DALES PONY
Origin: England

Long neck
Low withers
Short back
Small ears
Powerful hindquarters
Sloping shoulders
Strong, slender limbs
Feather on limbs

SHETLAND PONY
Origin: Scotland

Short, strong back
Short neck
Small ears
Deep, compact body
Small head
Long, sloping shoulders
Short, strong limbs

Dorsal stripe
Black and silver mane
Small ears
Low withers
Straight profile
Wide nostrils
Thick jowl
Dun coat
Broad, deep chest
Zebra-barred limbs

DARTMOOR PONY
Origin: England

Short, strong neck
Small ears
Small head
Low withers
Short back
Sloping croup
Long, thick mane
Long, sloping shoulders
Broad, deep chest
Deep, compact body
Long, thick tail
Strong, slender limbs
Short cannon bone
Feather on limbs

Ponies 2

Small ears

Short back

Deep, compact body

Thick mane

Short, strong limbs

Long, thick tail

Short cannon bone

ICELANDIC HORSE
Origin: Iceland

Broad forehead

Long, arched neck

Straight profile

Well-defined withers

Tapered muzzle

Wide nostrils

Toad (hooded) eye

Small ears

Thick mane

Long back

Sloping croup

Wide nostrils

Broad, deep chest

Thick tail

Broad, deep chest

Short cannon bone

Deep, compact body

Short, sturdy limbs

Sloping shoulders

EXMOOR PONY
Origin: England

Strong, slender limbs

Small ears

Long, thick mane

Deep, compact body

Small ears

Deep, compact body

Sloping shoulders

Long, sloping shoulders

Sloping croup

Short cannon bone

Short, sturdy limbs

Long, thick tail

Long, thick tail

FELL PONY
Origin: England

WELSH MOUNTAIN PONY
Origin: Wales

Small ears
Well-defined withers
Slim body
Sloping shoulders
Strong, slender limbs

CASPIAN PONY
Origin: Middle East

Small ears
Broad forehead
Wide nostrils
Deep chest
Long, flaxen mane
Short, strong back
Sloping croup
Deep, compact body
Long, flaxen tail
Short cannon bone

HAFLINGER PONY
Origin: Austria

Short, straight back
Sloping croup
Compact body
Long, thick tail

AUSTRALIAN PONY
Origin: Australia

Small ears
Thick mane
Black coat
Sloping croup
Broad, deep chest
Long, thick tail

ARIEGEOIS PONY
Origin: France

Small ears
Short neck
Well-defined withers
Straight shoulders
Long, thick tail

POTTOCK PONY
Origin: France

Small ears
Compact body
Sloping shoulders
Strong, slender limbs
Long cannon bone

HACKNEY PONY
Origin: England

Small ears
Well-defined withers
Sloping croup
Sloping shoulders
Short, sturdy limbs
Long, thick tail

LANDAIS PONY
Origin: France

31

Light horses 1

A LIGHT HORSE CAN BE DEFINED as any horse, other than a heavy horse or pony, whose size and conformation make it suitable for riding or driving. Most light horses are between 14.2 and 17.2 hands (147–178 cm) in height. The shape of their back – not too broad, with strong shoulders and well-defined withers – enables a saddle to be fitted easily. Some light horses, notably the Hanoverian, have long necks, long, sloping shoulders, powerful hindquarters, a smooth riding movement, and equable temperaments, which make them suitable as riding horses. Other light horses, such as the Frederiksborg, have fairly flat withers, short, upright necks, powerful, upright shoulders, and a high-stepping action, which make them more suitable as carriage horses. The oldest and most pure-bred of all the light horses is the Arab. This breed, together with the Barb and the Spanish horse (of which the Andalucian is a descendant), is thought to be the foundation of all light horse breeds, including the Thoroughbred, which is widely used for racing (see pp. 44-45).

Long neck

Well-defined withers

Long, sloping shoulders

Short, upright neck

Powerful, upright shoulders

Flat withers

Strong back

High-set tail

Powerful hindquarters

Long body

Chestnut coat

FREDERIKSBORG
Origin: Denmark

Strong neck

Deep, wide body

Powerful hindquarters

Powerful shoulders

Clean limbs, without feather

CLEVELAND BAY
Origin: England

Short, thick neck

Deep body

High-set tail

White coat

Powerful hindquarters

Short, strong limbs

LIPIZZANER
Origin: Slovenia

Prominent joints

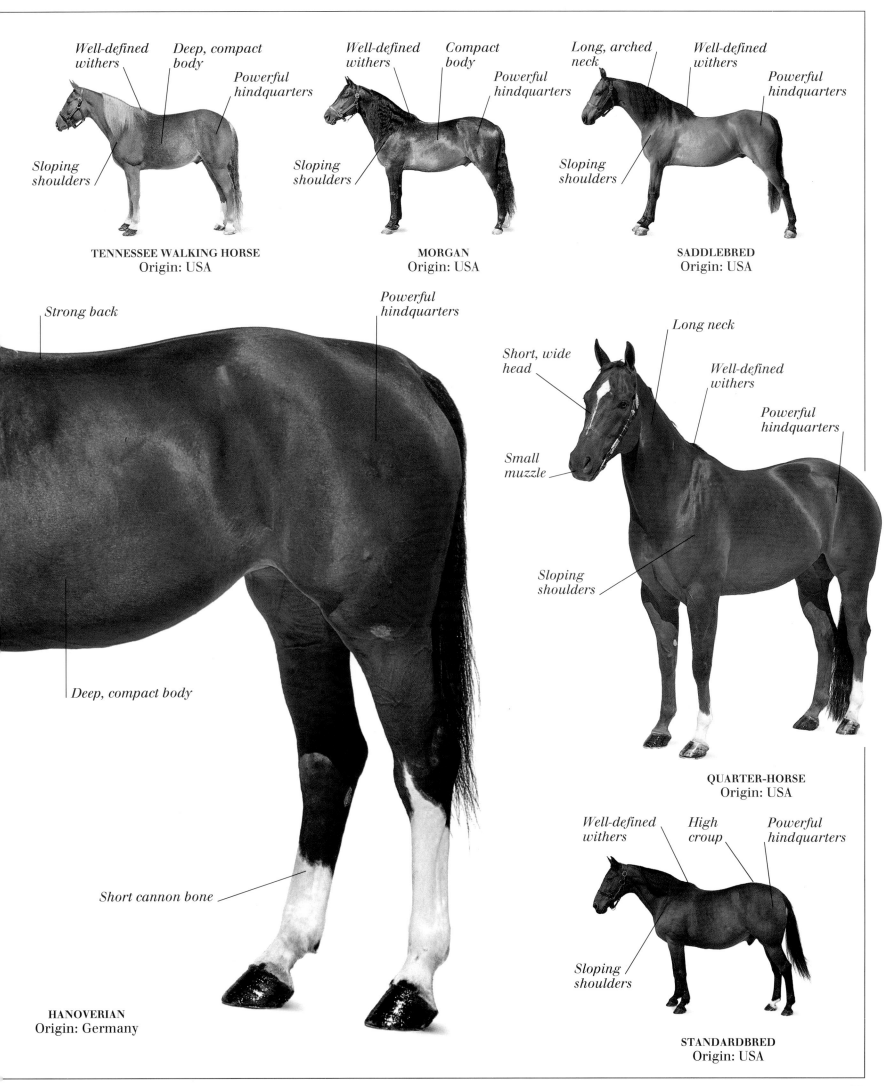

TENNESSEE WALKING HORSE
Origin: USA

Well-defined withers

Deep, compact body

Powerful hindquarters

Sloping shoulders

MORGAN
Origin: USA

Well-defined withers

Compact body

Powerful hindquarters

Sloping shoulders

SADDLEBRED
Origin: USA

Long, arched neck

Well-defined withers

Powerful hindquarters

Sloping shoulders

Strong back

Powerful hindquarters

Deep, compact body

Short cannon bone

HANOVERIAN
Origin: Germany

Short, wide head

Long neck

Well-defined withers

Powerful hindquarters

Small muzzle

Sloping shoulders

QUARTER-HORSE
Origin: USA

Well-defined withers

High croup

Powerful hindquarters

Sloping shoulders

STANDARDBRED
Origin: USA

Light horses 2

Fine,
silky tail

Powerful
hindquarters

Short
back

Well-defined
withers

Concave
profile

Sloping
shoulders

Compact
body

Flat
knees

Short
cannon bone

ARAB
Origin: Middle East

Powerful
hindquarters

Long,
narrow
body

Long
neck

Sloping
shoulders

AKHAL-TEKE
Origin: Turkmenistan

Straight
back

Strong
neck

Powerful
hindquarters

Sickle-
shaped
hind limb

Upright
shoulders

KABARDIN
Origin: Northern Caucasus

Powerful
hindquarters

Compact
body

Sloping
shoulders

SHAGYA-ARAB
Origin: Hungary

Powerful
hindquarters

Compact
body

Well-defined
withers

Sloping
shoulders

ANGLO-ARAB
Origins: UK and France

High croup

Powerful
hindquarters

Short,
strong back

Strong
neck

Upright
shoulders

Deep, compact
body

BARB
Origin: Morocco

Powerful hindquarters

Wide, straight back

Short, upright shoulders

DON
Origin: Russian Federation

Powerful hindquarters

Well-defined withers

Sloping shoulders

Short cannon bone

TRAKEHNER
Origin: Poland

Powerful hindquarters

Short, straight back

Well-defined withers

Short, sloping shoulders

BUDENNY
Origin: Russian Federation

Powerful hindquarters

Compact body

Sloping shoulders

TERSK
Origin: Northern Caucasus

Powerful hindquarters

Strong back

Well-defined withers

Sloping shoulders

NONIUS
Origin: Hungary

Powerful hindquarters

Short, strong back

Sloping shoulders

Short cannon bone

DUTCH WARMBLOOD
Origin: Netherlands

Powerful hindquarters

Compact body

Strong neck

Upright shoulders

FRENCH TROTTER
Origin: France

Powerful hindquarters

Well-defined withers

Long neck

Sloping shoulders

SELLE FRANCAIS
Origin: France

Powerful hindquarters

Strong, arched neck

Long, wavy mane

Strong, sloping shoulders

Compact body

ANDALUCIAN
Origin: Spain

Heavy horses 1

HEAVY HORSES ARE LARGE, POWERFUL HORSES that have been used in agriculture and for hauling heavy loads. They typically stand between 14.2 and 18 hands high (147–183 cm), and some of the larger breeds – the Shire, for example – may weigh as much as 1,000 kg (2,200 lb). Heavy horses are characterized by relatively short backs and limbs; broad, powerful chests; good temperaments; and great strength and stamina. They grow a thick winter coat that is shed in summer. Some heavy horses have fine hair (known as feather) on their lower limbs. They are generally easily managed and have been put to a variety of uses. Heavy horses were traditionally used in warfare, and modern breeds are thought to be descended from horses that were used for carrying heavily armoured medieval knights into battle. More recently, heavy horses such as the Percheron (see pp. 38-39) were used in World War I to pull supply wagons and heavy artillery. Heavy horses have also been used for various types of agricultural work, particularly ploughing. In industry, they were used for hauling loads such as goods wagons and barges. The work previously carried out by heavy horses is now done mostly by machines, although they are sometimes still used in farming and for pulling brewer's drays.

Short back

Sloping croup

Wide, powerful hindquarters

Wide, powerful body

Powerful, sturdy limbs

Heavy feather on limbs

SHIRE
Origin: England

Powerful, arched neck

Low, broad withers

Broad forehead

Deep, rounded body

Broad, powerful chest

Light feather on limbs

Powerful, sturdy limbs

SUFFOLK PUNCH
Origin: England

Powerful neck

Well-defined withers

Straight profile

Powerful hindquarters

Broad, powerful chest

Heavy feather on limbs

Powerful, sturdy limbs

CLYDESDALE
Origin: Scotland

Long, powerful neck

Low, broad withers

Broad forehead

Roman (convex) nose

Wide, deep shoulders

Broad, powerful chest

Forelimbs set well apart

Long cannon bone

Powerful hindquarters

Powerful, arched neck

Straight profile

Light feather on limbs

Broad, powerful chest

Powerful, short limbs

BRETON
Origin: France

Powerful, arched neck

Straight profile

Low, wide withers

Powerful, short limbs

Long, sloping shoulders

Light feather on limbs

Short cannon bone

BOULONNAIS
Origin: France

Short, strong back

Powerful, arched neck

Powerful hindquarters

Broad, powerful chest

Powerful, sturdy limbs

Forelimbs set well apart

Light feather on limbs

BRABANT
Origin: Belgium

Powerful hindquarters

Short, strong back

Powerful neck

Broad, powerful chest

Powerful, sturdy limbs

NORMAN COB
Origin: France

Short, flat back

Powerful neck

Powerful hindquarters

Deep, powerful chest

Powerful, sturdy limbs

Forelimbs set well apart

Light feather on limbs

ITALIAN HEAVY DRAUGHT
Origin: Italy

Powerful, thick neck

Deep, rounded body

Powerful hindquarters

Broad, powerful chest

Heavy feather on limbs

Powerful, sturdy limbs

JUTLAND
Origin: Denmark

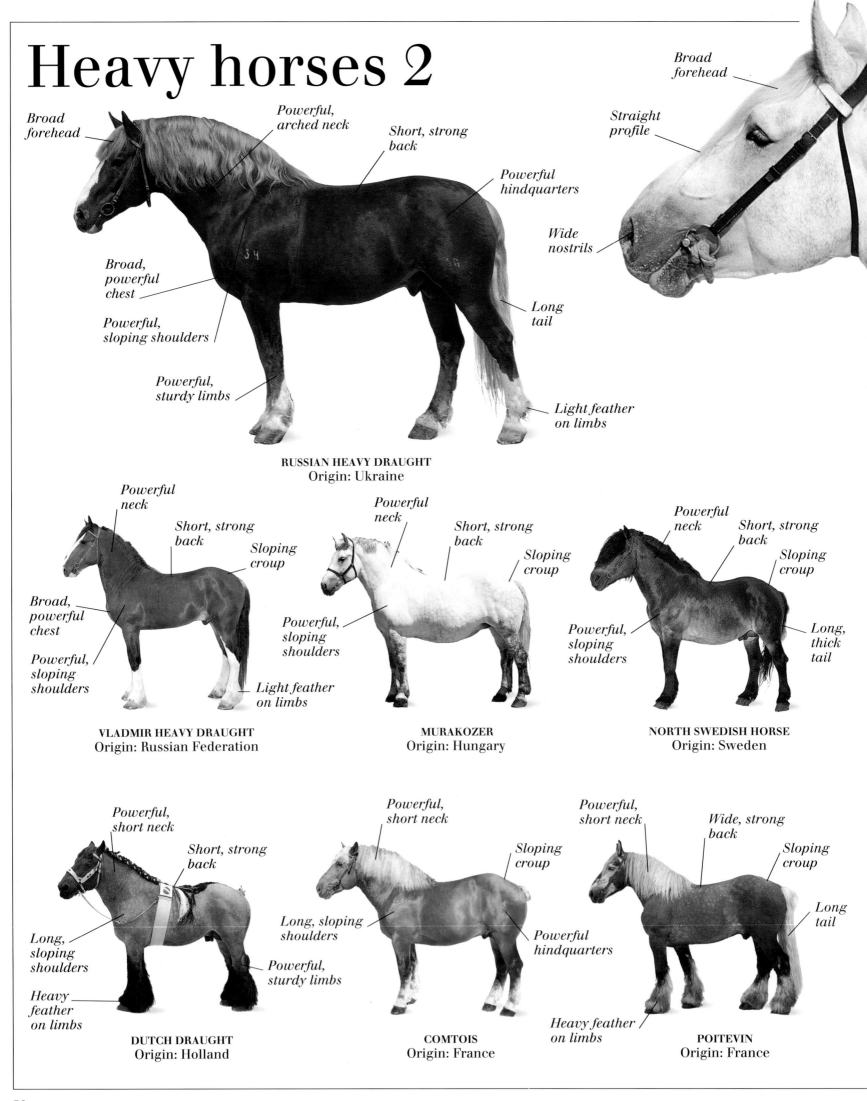

Heavy horses 2

Broad forehead

Powerful, arched neck

Short, strong back

Powerful hindquarters

Broad forehead

Straight profile

Wide nostrils

Broad, powerful chest

Powerful, sloping shoulders

Long tail

Powerful, sturdy limbs

Light feather on limbs

RUSSIAN HEAVY DRAUGHT
Origin: Ukraine

Powerful neck

Short, strong back

Sloping croup

Broad, powerful chest

Powerful, sloping shoulders

Light feather on limbs

VLADMIR HEAVY DRAUGHT
Origin: Russian Federation

Powerful neck

Short, strong back

Sloping croup

Powerful, sloping shoulders

MURAKOZER
Origin: Hungary

Powerful neck

Short, strong back

Sloping croup

Powerful, sloping shoulders

Long, thick tail

NORTH SWEDISH HORSE
Origin: Sweden

Powerful, short neck

Short, strong back

Long, sloping shoulders

Powerful, sturdy limbs

Heavy feather on limbs

DUTCH DRAUGHT
Origin: Holland

Powerful, short neck

Sloping croup

Long, sloping shoulders

Powerful hindquarters

COMTOIS
Origin: France

Powerful, short neck

Wide, strong back

Sloping croup

Long tail

Heavy feather on limbs

POITEVIN
Origin: France

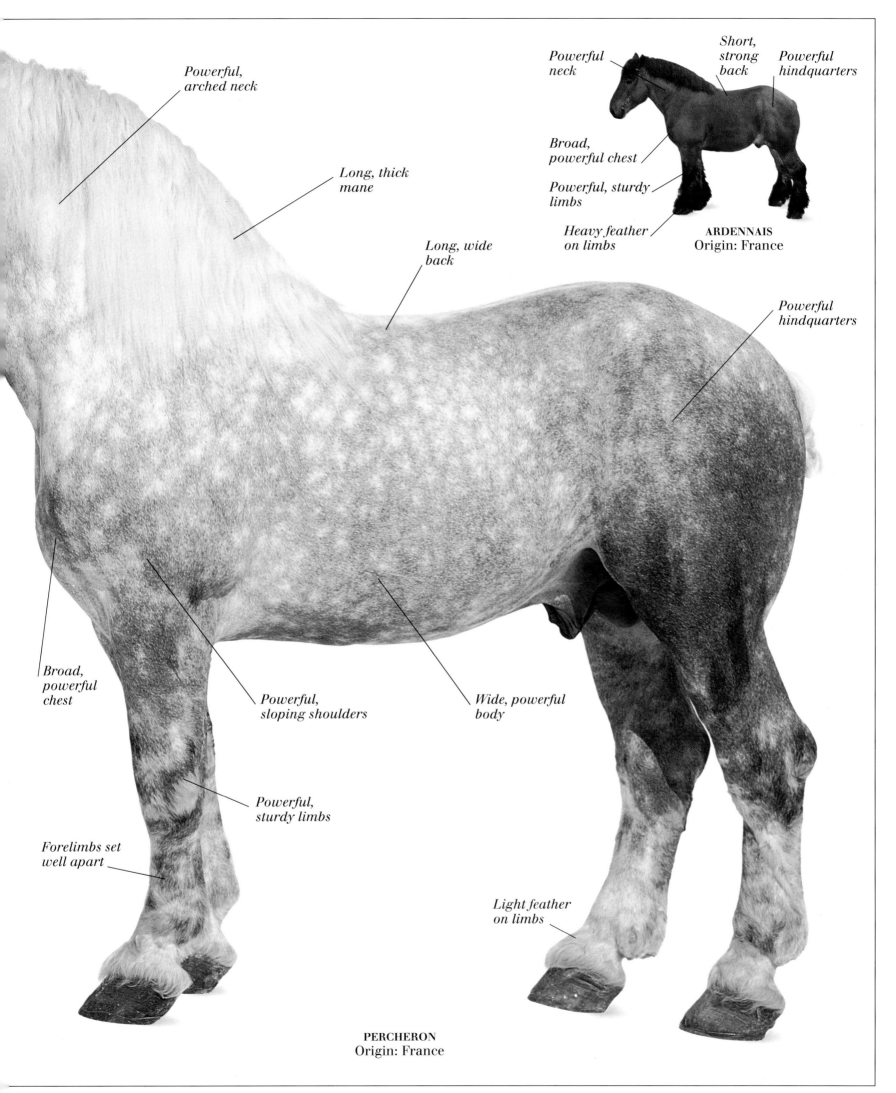

Powerful,
arched neck

Long, thick
mane

Long, wide
back

Broad,
powerful chest

Powerful,
sturdy
limbs

Heavy feather
on limbs

Powerful
neck

Short,
strong
back

Powerful
hindquarters

ARDENNAIS
Origin: France

Powerful
hindquarters

Broad,
powerful
chest

Powerful,
sloping shoulders

Wide, powerful
body

Powerful,
sturdy limbs

Forelimbs set
well apart

Light feather
on limbs

PERCHERON
Origin: France

Gait

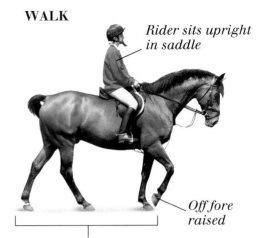

Rider sits upright in saddle

THE HORSE HAS FOUR NATURAL GAITS (PACES): walk, trot, canter, and gallop. The walk is a four-beat gait – four footfalls (beats) can be heard in each stride. Each stride is of equal length, and at least two feet are on the ground at the same time. The sequence of footfalls while walking (beginning with the near hind leg) is: near hind, near fore, off hind, and off fore. The trot is a two-beat gait in which the legs move as two diagonal pairs. The first beat occurs as the near fore and off hind touch the ground (the left diagonal). The second beat occurs as the off fore and near hind touch the ground (the right diagonal). The canter is a three-beat gait with a moment of suspension when all four feet are off the ground. The sequence of footfalls while cantering (beginning with the near hind leg) is: near hind, near fore and off hind (the left diagonal), and off fore. The gallop is the horse's fastest pace and is a four-beat gait. The sequence of footfalls while galloping (beginning with the near hind leg) is: near hind, off hind, near fore, and off fore, followed by a period of suspension with all feet off the ground. As well as the natural gaits, there are various specialized gaits, such as pacing. Most common in harness racing, pacing has two beats, with the legs moving in lateral pairs: near fore and near hind, followed by off fore and off hind.

PACING IN HARNESS RACING

Off fore raised

Near hind, off hind, and near fore on ground

TROT

Rider sits upright in saddle

Off fore raised

Near hind raised | *Off hind on ground* | *Near fore on ground*

CANTER

Rider sits upright in saddle

Near hind raised

Off hind on ground

Off fore and near fore raised

Rider sits upright in saddle

Near hind on ground

Off hind raised

Near fore on ground

Off fore raised

Rider sits upright in saddle

Near hind raised

Off hind and near fore on ground

Off fore raised

GALLOP

Rider leans forwards in saddle

Off hind raised

Near hind coming down

Near fore and off fore raised

Rider leans forwards out of saddle

Off hind on ground

Near hind and off fore on ground

Near fore raised

Rider leans forwards out of saddle

Off hind raised

Near hind and off fore on ground

Near fore raised

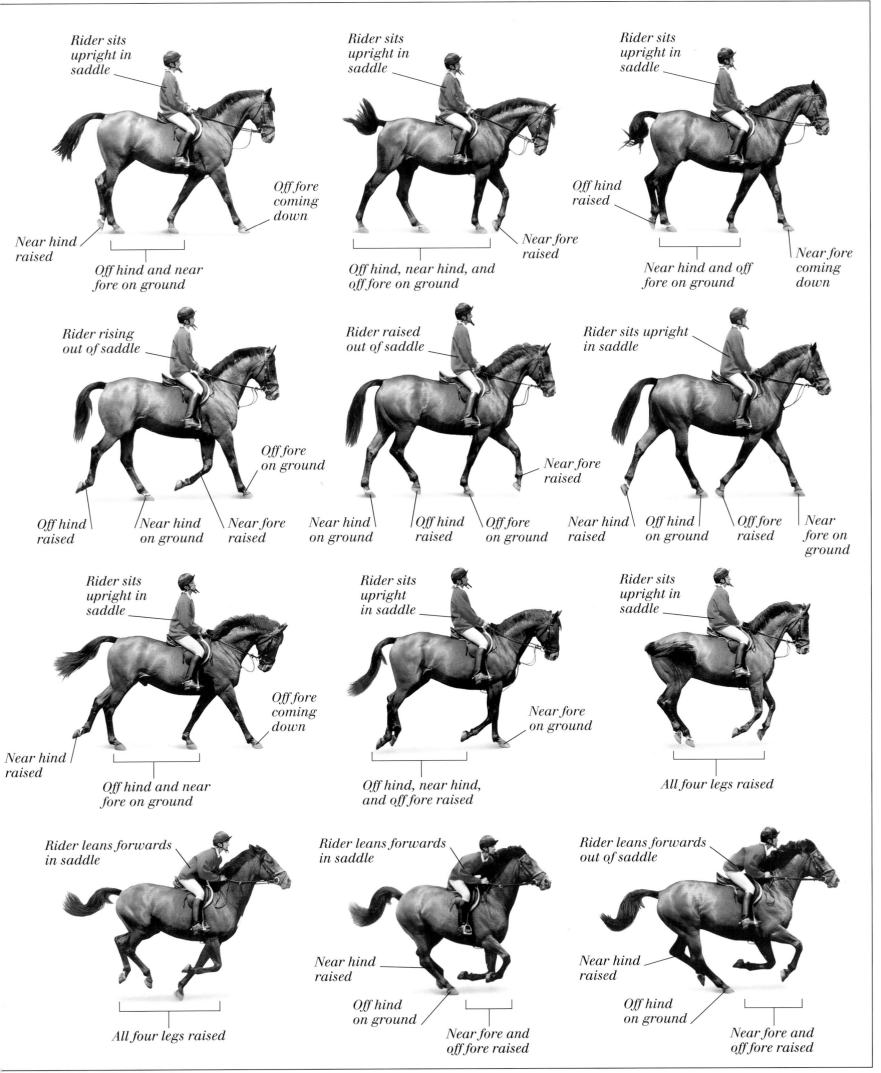

Rider sits upright in saddle

Near hind raised

Off fore coming down

Off hind and near fore on ground

Rider sits upright in saddle

Off hind, near hind, and off fore on ground

Near fore raised

Rider sits upright in saddle

Off hind raised

Near hind and off fore on ground

Near fore coming down

Rider rising out of saddle

Off fore on ground

Off hind raised

Near hind on ground

Near fore raised

Rider raised out of saddle

Near hind on ground

Off hind raised

Off fore on ground

Near fore raised

Rider sits upright in saddle

Near hind raised

Off hind on ground

Off fore raised

Near fore on ground

Rider sits upright in saddle

Near hind raised

Off hind and near fore on ground

Off fore coming down

Rider sits upright in saddle

Off hind, near hind, and off fore raised

Near fore on ground

Rider sits upright in saddle

All four legs raised

Rider leans forwards in saddle

All four legs raised

Rider leans forwards in saddle

Near hind raised

Off hind on ground

Near fore and off fore raised

Rider leans forwards out of saddle

Near hind raised

Off hind on ground

Near fore and off fore raised

Jumping

JUMPING IS AN IMPORTANT PART of many equestrian sports, such as showjumping and eventing, which includes cross-country jumping. In cross-country jumping, the course is usually designed to take advantage of the natural terrain, including features such as water and ditches. Water-jumps are among

HORSE AND RIDER JUMPING FENCE

the most difficult obstacles because they often involve several stages; for example, the horse may have to jump over a fence in the water and then jump out of the water on to a sloping bank. There are two main types of showjumping fence: uprights, such as basic upright planks, poles, and walls; and spreads, such as triple bars, hog's-backs, and parallel poles. Uprights are typically between 0.9 m (3 ft) and 1.8 m (6 ft) high, and spreads between 0.8 m (2 ft 6 in) and

2 m (6 ft 6 in) wide. Most showjumping fences consist of wooden stands, known as wings, that support poles or planks. Some parts of the fence – poles, for example – are designed to fall down on impact, to prevent injury to the horse and rider. On the approach to any fence, the horse balances itself and then thrusts forwards and upwards with its hind legs. As the horse clears the fence, its legs are folded under its body, with its head and neck stretched to their full extent. The rider leans forwards and allows the horse to move its head and neck freely, to avoid impeding its natural jumping action. The horse lands first on one foreleg, then regains its balance as its other legs reach the ground.

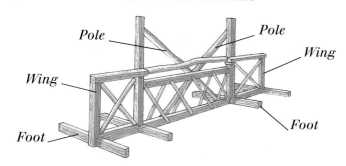

EXAMPLES OF FENCES

Pole · Pole · Wing · Wing · Foot · Foot

**RUSTIC UPRIGHT WITH CROSS POLES
(SHOWJUMPING)**

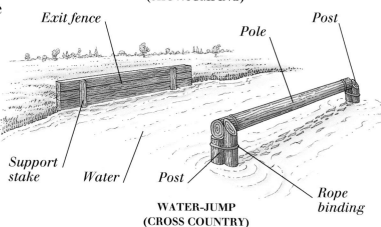

Exit fence · Pole · Post · Support stake · Water · Post · Rope binding

**WATER-JUMP
(CROSS COUNTRY)**

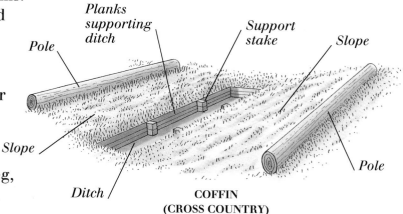

Planks supporting ditch · Support stake · Slope · Pole · Slope · Ditch · Pole

**COFFIN
(CROSS COUNTRY)**

HORSE JUMPING A PARALLEL FENCE

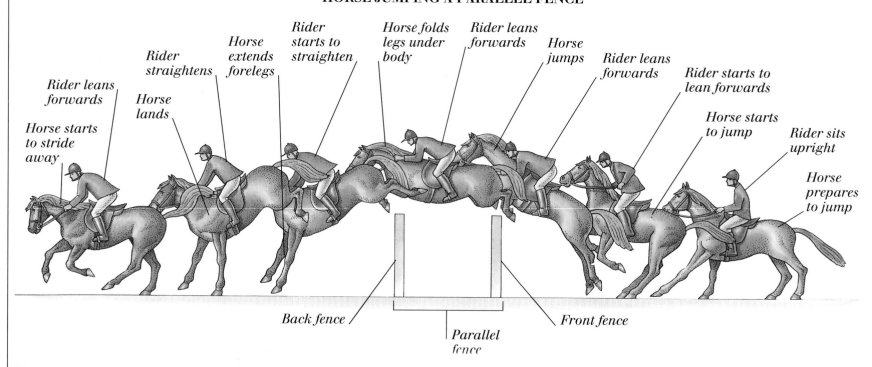

Rider straightens · Horse extends forelegs · Rider starts to straighten · Horse folds legs under body · Rider leans forwards · Horse jumps · Rider leans forwards · Rider starts to lean forwards

Rider leans forwards · Horse lands · Horse starts to jump · Rider sits upright

Horse starts to stride away · Horse prepares to jump

Back fence · Front fence · Parallel fence

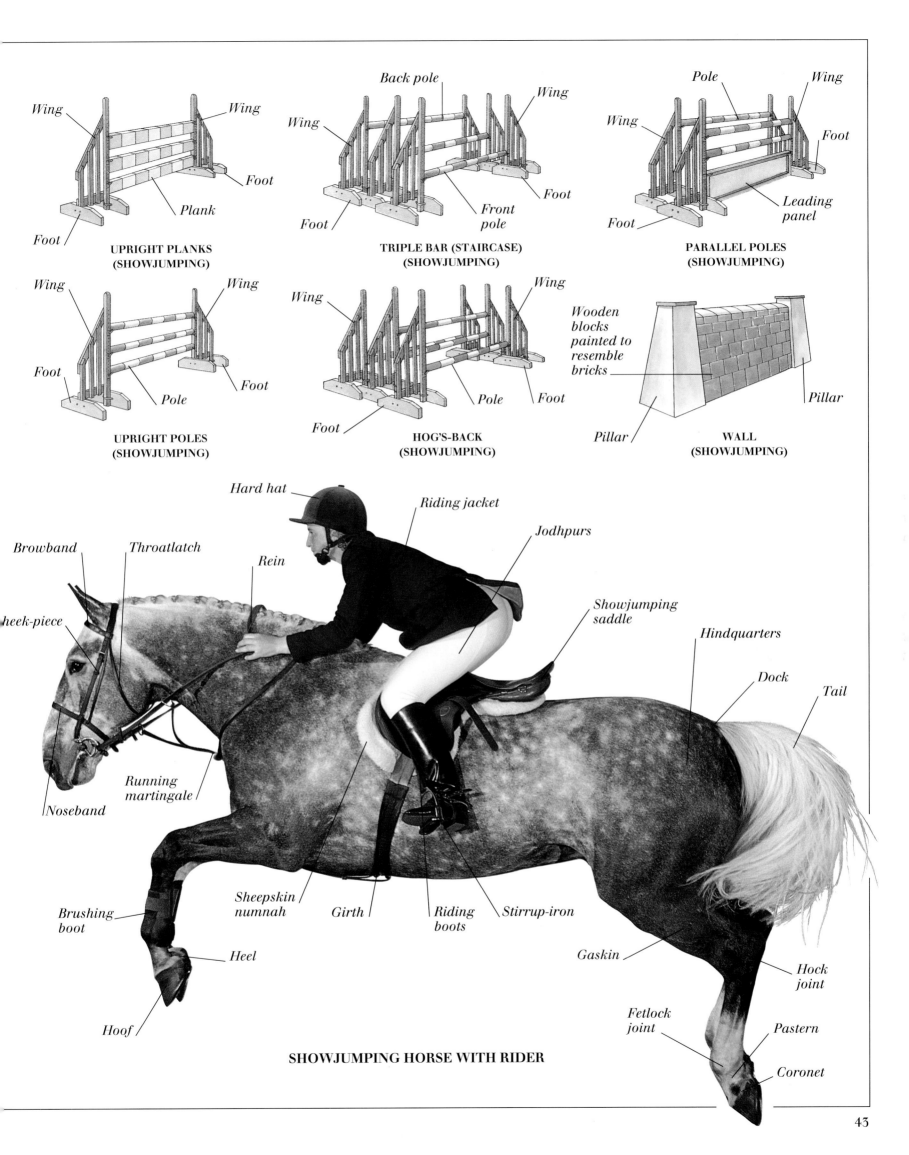

**UPRIGHT PLANKS
(SHOWJUMPING)**

Wing
Wing
Foot
Plank
Foot

**TRIPLE BAR (STAIRCASE)
(SHOWJUMPING)**

Back pole
Wing
Wing
Foot
Front
pole
Foot

**PARALLEL POLES
(SHOWJUMPING)**

Pole
Wing
Wing
Foot
Leading
panel
Foot

**UPRIGHT POLES
(SHOWJUMPING)**

Wing
Wing
Foot
Foot
Pole

**HOG'S-BACK
(SHOWJUMPING)**

Wing
Wing
Foot
Pole
Foot

**WALL
(SHOWJUMPING)**

Wooden
blocks
painted to
resemble
bricks
Pillar
Pillar

Hard hat
Riding jacket
Jodhpurs
Browband
Throatlatch
Rein
Showjumping
saddle
heek-piece
Hindquarters
Dock
Tail
Noseband
Running
martingale
Brushing
boot
Sheepskin
numnah
Girth
Riding
boots
Stirrup-iron
Gaskin
Heel
Hock
joint
Hoof
Fetlock
joint
Pastern
Coronet

SHOWJUMPING HORSE WITH RIDER

Racing

FROM ANCIENT GREEK TIMES TO THE PRESENT DAY, horse-racing has been one of the most popular equine sports. Modern horse-racing takes several different forms. The simplest is flat-racing, in which jockeys ride horses that race against each other over a course without jumps. Races with jumps are divided into two types: steeplechases and hurdle-races. In steeplechases, the fences are 137 cm (4 ft 6 in) high and over. In hurdle-races, the fences are 107 cm (3 ft 6 in) high and over, and are flexible, so that they bend if a horse hits them when jumping. In flat-races, steeplechases, and hurdle-races, Thoroughbred horses are used. This breed has been developed to have the strength and stamina to gallop fast over courses with or without jumps. In shorter flat-races, horses may reach speeds of about 65 kilometres per hour (40 miles per hour). Harness racing requires a breed of horse that can pace or trot (see pp. 40-41) while pulling a sulky (a lightweight, two-wheeled cart). Breeds such as the Standardbred and the French Trotter have been developed especially for this type of racing. In pacing races the horses wear hobbles to prevent them from breaking into a gallop or trot. When racing, jockeys and drivers wear a set of silks, comprising a jacket and cap in a particular pattern and colour combination. Each racehorse owner has a specific pattern and colour combination for his or her silks, so that the horse and its owner can be identified easily.

RACEHORSE AND JOCKEY

Headpiece
Throatlatch
Ear
Forelock
Browband
Eye
Cheek-piece
Nostril
Irish martingale
Muzzle
Loose-ring snaffle bit

HARNESS RACING WITH A STANDARDBRED HORSE

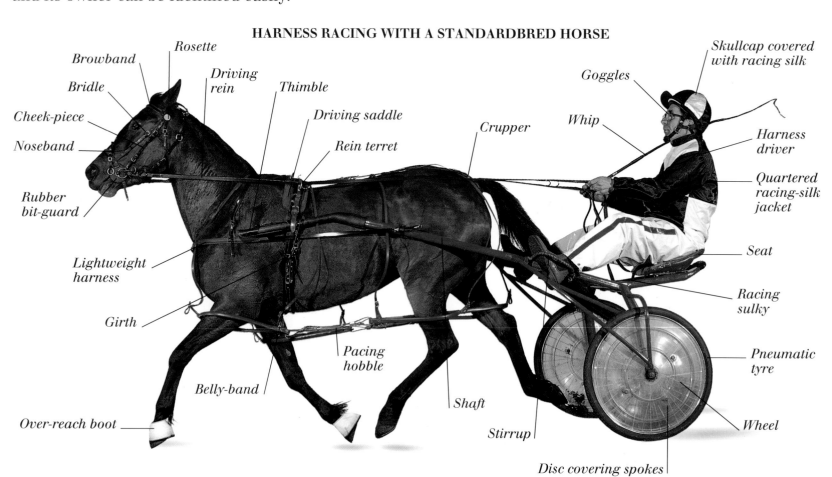

Rosette
Browband
Driving rein
Bridle
Thimble
Cheek-piece
Driving saddle
Noseband
Rein terret
Rubber bit-guard
Crupper
Goggles
Whip
Skullcap covered with racing silk
Harness driver
Quartered racing-silk jacket
Seat
Lightweight harness
Racing sulky
Girth
Pacing hobble
Pneumatic tyre
Belly-band
Shaft
Over-reach boot
Stirrup
Wheel
Disc covering spokes

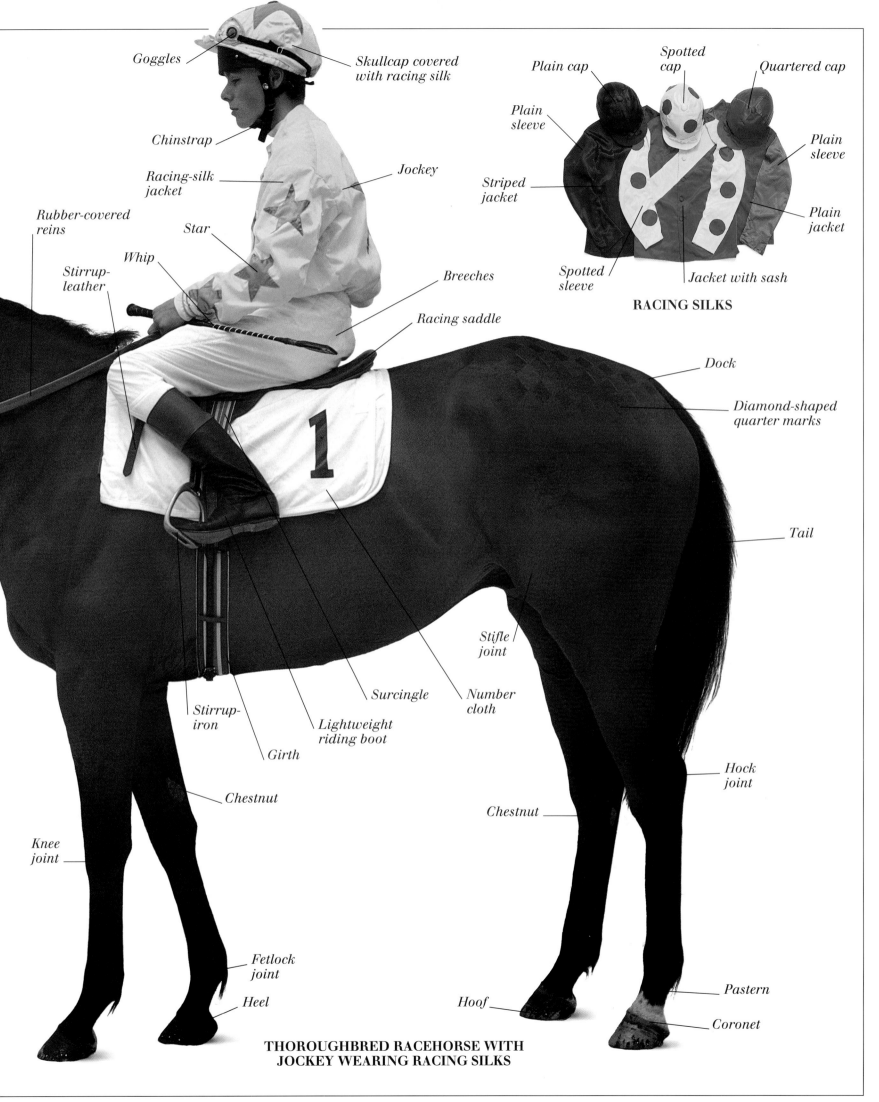

Goggles

Skullcap covered
with racing silk

Chinstrap

Racing-silk
jacket

Jockey

Rubber-covered
reins

Star

Whip

Stirrup-
leather

Breeches

Racing saddle

Stirrup-
iron

Girth

Lightweight
riding boot

Surcingle

Number
cloth

Stifle
joint

Chestnut

Knee
joint

Fetlock
joint

Heel

Hoof

Coronet

Pastern

Chestnut

Hock
joint

Tail

Diamond-shaped
quarter marks

Dock

RACING SILKS

Plain cap

Spotted
cap

Quartered cap

Plain
sleeve

Plain
sleeve

Striped
jacket

Plain
jacket

Spotted
sleeve

Jacket with sash

**THOROUGHBRED RACEHORSE WITH
JOCKEY WEARING RACING SILKS**

Harnesses 1

HARNESS IS THE GENERAL TERM FOR THE EQUIPMENT that enables a horse to pull a load, such as a wagon, carriage, or plough. Most harnesses have three basic components: a bridle, collar, and breeching. The bridle is a set of straps that fits over the horse's head. Reins are attached to the bridle to enable the driver to control the horse. The collar is worn around the horse's neck or breast and is attached to the load by leather or chain traces. As the horse moves forwards, it pushes against the collar to pull the load. The breeching is a set of one or more straps that fits on the horse's hindquarters. The most important component, called the breeching strap, fits behind the horse's hindquarters and enables it to brake or to reverse whatever it is pulling. There are many variations to these components, each adapted for a different function. For instance, bridles that are fitted with blinkers – known as closed bridles – prevent horses from seeing anything approaching from behind or the sides, which could otherwise frighten them. Teams of two or more horses are harnessed in a different way from a horse working alone. For example, a pair of horses hitched to a wagon is usually positioned with one horse on each side of the wagon's central pole; each horse is attached by chains to the pole. However, a single horse pulling a wagon is usually hitched between two shafts, which are attached to the horse's collar by traces.

A PAIR OF SHIRES PULLING A DRAY

A PAIR OF SHIRES HARNESSED TO A PLOUGH

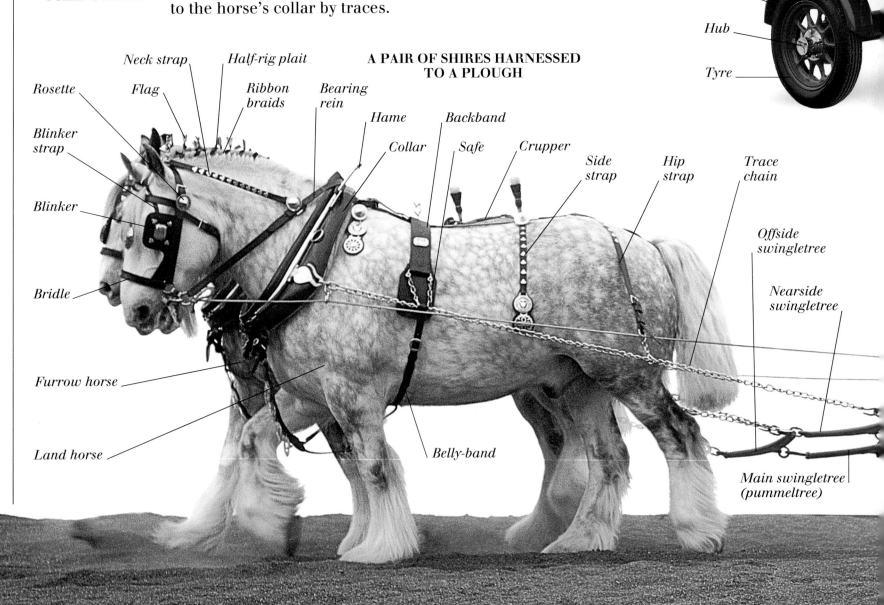

Dray

Mudguard

Hub

Tyre

Neck strap

Half-rig plait

Rosette

Flag

Ribbon braids

Bearing rein

Blinker strap

Hame

Backband

Collar

Safe

Crupper

Blinker

Side strap

Hip strap

Trace chain

Bridle

Offside swingletree

Nearside swingletree

Furrow horse

Land horse

Belly-band

Main swingletree (pummeltree)

A PAIR OF SHIRES HARNESSED TO A DRAY

Rein terret

Driving pad

Hip strap

Offside draught rein

Fly-head terret

Face-piece

Fixed-cheek Liverpool bit

Footrest

Housen

Seat

Crupper

Hame

Hame eye

Loin strap

Offside coupling rein

Billet

Cross-head

Hame chain

Buckle

Pole

Horse brass

Trace chain

Pole chain

Roller bolt

Axle

Splinter bar

Girth

Hame hook

False martingale

Breeching strap

Ploughman

Plough bridle (hake)

Land wheel

Furrow wheel

Plough line

Ploughshare

Handle

Beam

Stays

Stilt

Coulter

Land-side plate

Mould-board

Harnesses 2

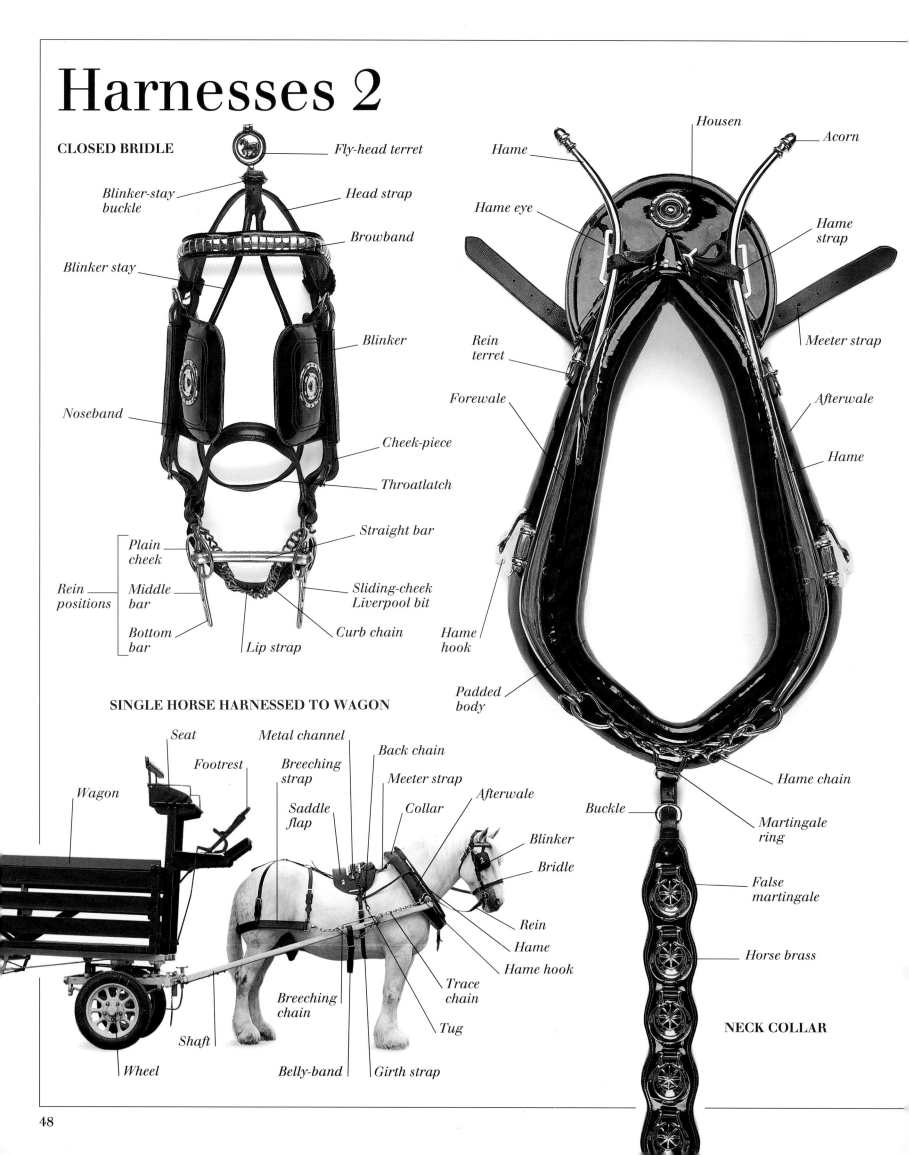

CLOSED BRIDLE

- Fly-head terret
- Blinker-stay buckle
- Head strap
- Browband
- Blinker stay
- Blinker
- Noseband
- Cheek-piece
- Throatlatch
- Straight bar
- Plain cheek
- Middle bar
- Rein positions
- Sliding-cheek Liverpool bit
- Bottom bar
- Lip strap
- Curb chain

SINGLE HORSE HARNESSED TO WAGON

- Seat
- Metal channel
- Back chain
- Footrest
- Breeching strap
- Meeter strap
- Wagon
- Saddle flap
- Collar
- Afterwale
- Blinker
- Bridle
- Rein
- Hame
- Hame hook
- Trace chain
- Breeching chain
- Tug
- Shaft
- Wheel
- Belly-band
- Girth strap

NECK COLLAR

- Housen
- Acorn
- Hame
- Hame strap
- Hame eye
- Meeter strap
- Rein terret
- Afterwale
- Forewale
- Hame
- Hame hook
- Padded body
- Buckle
- Hame chain
- Martingale ring
- False martingale
- Horse brass

48

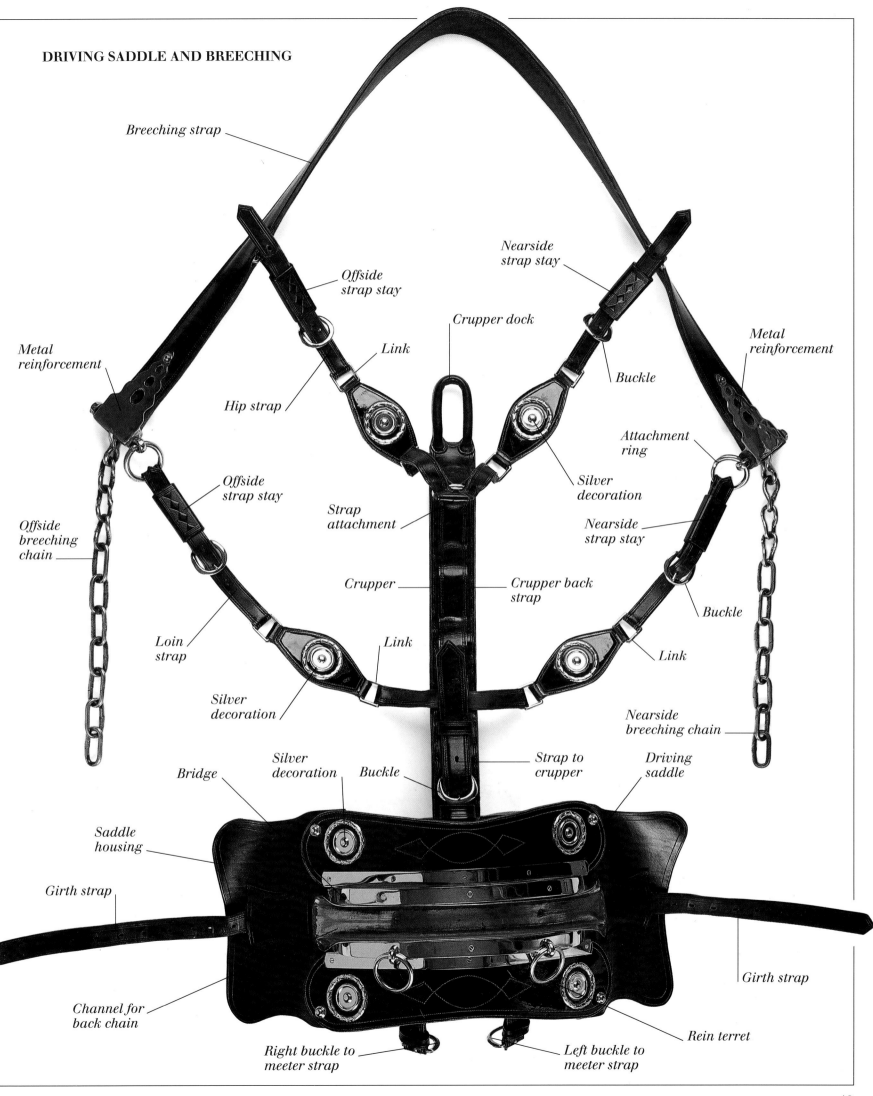

DRIVING SADDLE AND BREECHING

Breeching strap

Offside strap stay

Nearside strap stay

Crupper dock

Link

Metal reinforcement

Hip strap

Buckle

Metal reinforcement

Attachment ring

Offside strap stay

Silver decoration

Strap attachment

Nearside strap stay

Offside breeching chain

Crupper

Crupper back strap

Buckle

Loin strap

Link

Link

Silver decoration

Nearside breeching chain

Silver decoration

Strap to crupper

Driving saddle

Bridge

Buckle

Saddle housing

Girth strap

Girth strap

Channel for back chain

Rein terret

Right buckle to meeter strap

Left buckle to meeter strap

Bits and bridles

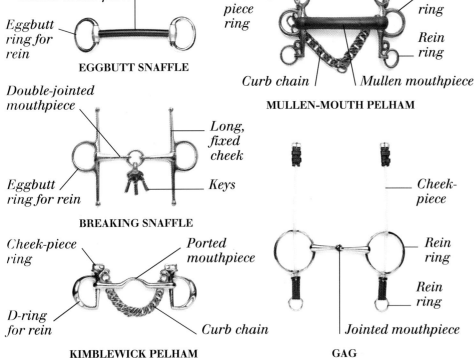

BITS AND BRIDLES ARE USED TO REGULATE the position of the horse's head, and to help control the pace and direction of the horse. A bit is the part of the bridle that is fitted into the horse's mouth over the tongue. Most bits are made of metal (usually stainless steel), although the mouthpiece may be covered in rubber or vulcanite. The mouthpiece may be straight, mullen (half-moon), jointed, or ported (with a hump in the middle). Bridles typically consist of a headpiece, and reins that are attached to the bit. There are various types of bridle, including double, snaffle, and Western bridles. The double bridle has two sets of reins and two bits – a curb bit and a snaffle bit (the snaffle bit is known as a bridoon when used in this way). The snaffle bridle has one set of reins and a snaffle bit. The Western bridle usually has one set of open-ended reins and a curb bit.

BRIDLING A HORSE

EXAMPLES OF BITS

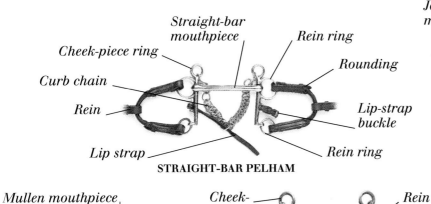

Straight-bar mouthpiece
Cheek-piece ring
Curb chain
Rein
Rein ring
Rounding
Lip-strap buckle
Lip strap
Rein ring

STRAIGHT-BAR PELHAM

Mullen mouthpiece
Eggbutt ring for rein

EGGBUTT SNAFFLE

Cheek-piece ring
Rein ring
Rein ring
Curb chain
Mullen mouthpiece

MULLEN-MOUTH PELHAM

Double-jointed mouthpiece
Long, fixed cheek
Eggbutt ring for rein
Keys

BREAKING SNAFFLE

Cheek-piece ring
Ported mouthpiece
D-ring for rein
Curb chain

KIMBLEWICK PELHAM

Cheek-piece
Rein ring
Rein ring
Jointed mouthpiece

GAG

DOUBLE BRIDLE

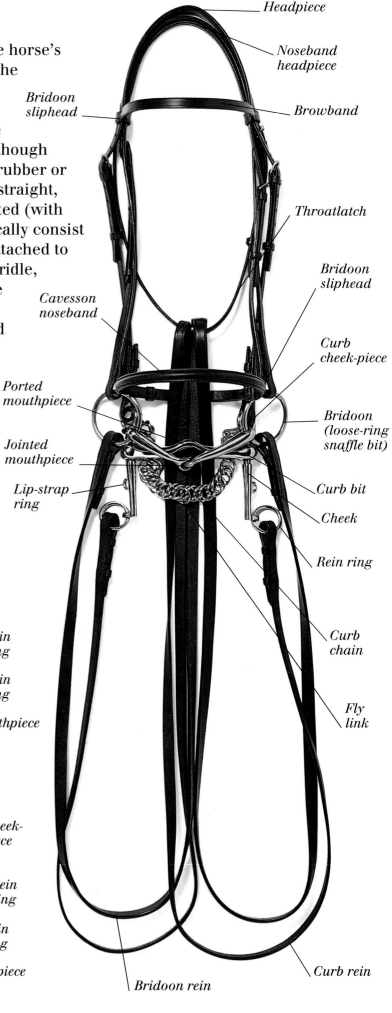

Headpiece
Noseband headpiece
Bridoon sliphead
Browband
Throatlatch
Bridoon sliphead
Cavesson noseband
Curb cheek-piece
Ported mouthpiece
Bridoon (loose-ring snaffle bit)
Jointed mouthpiece
Curb bit
Lip-strap ring
Cheek
Rein ring
Curb chain
Fly link
Curb rein
Bridoon rein

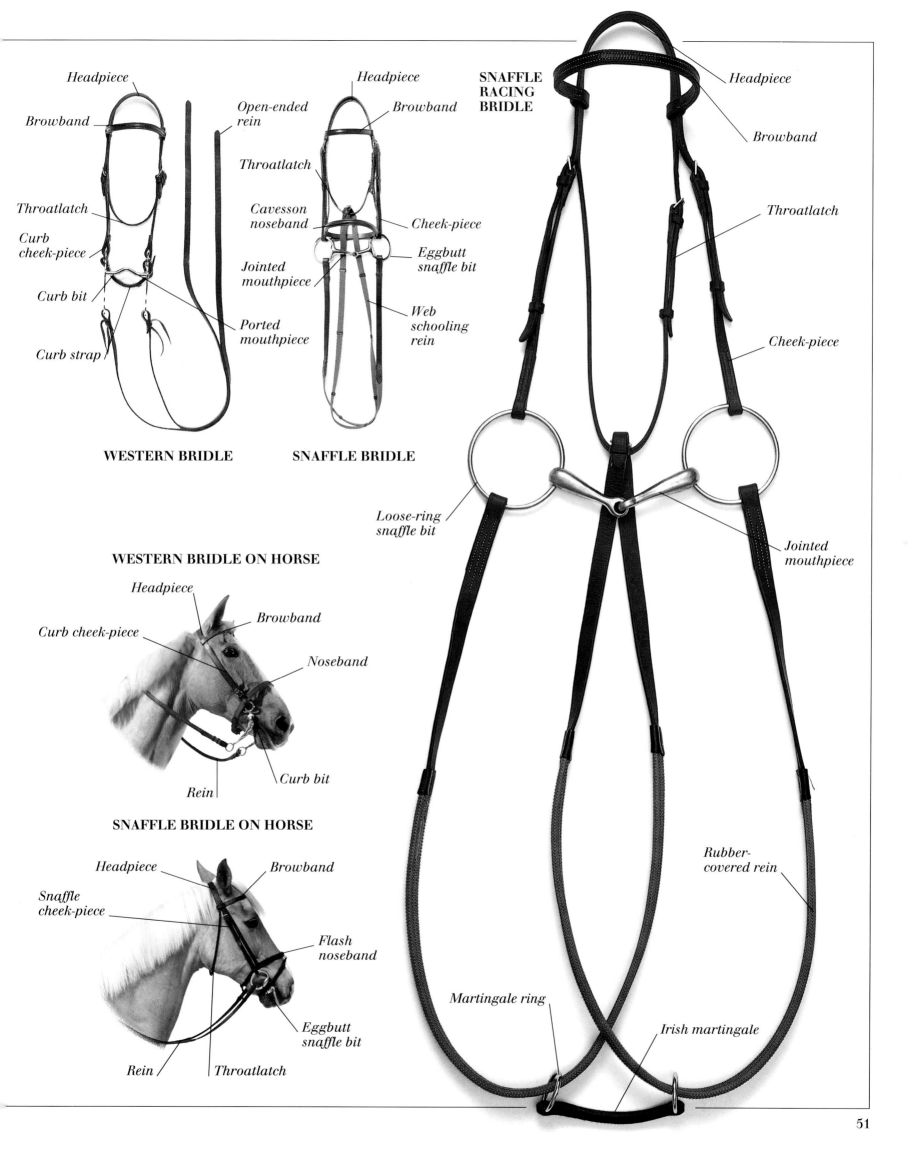

Headpiece

Browband

Throatlatch

*Curb
cheek-piece*

Curb bit

Curb strap

*Open-ended
rein*

WESTERN BRIDLE

Headpiece

Browband

Throatlatch

*Cavesson
noseband*

*Jointed
mouthpiece*

*Ported
mouthpiece*

Cheek-piece

*Eggbutt
snaffle bit*

*Web
schooling
rein*

SNAFFLE BRIDLE

**SNAFFLE
RACING
BRIDLE**

Headpiece

Browband

Throatlatch

Cheek-piece

*Loose-ring
snaffle bit*

*Jointed
mouthpiece*

*Rubber-
covered rein*

Martingale ring

Irish martingale

WESTERN BRIDLE ON HORSE

Headpiece

Curb cheek-piece

Browband

Noseband

Curb bit

Rein

SNAFFLE BRIDLE ON HORSE

Headpiece

*Snaffle
cheek-piece*

Browband

*Flash
noseband*

*Eggbutt
snaffle bit*

Rein

Throatlatch

Saddles

A SADDLE MAKES RIDING COMFORTABLE and safer for both the rider and the horse. It enables the rider to sit on the horse securely and to move freely, and it also helps to protect the horse. A saddle is built on a strong frame called a tree. On the underside of the saddle there is a channel called a gullet, which runs along the centre and fits over the horse's spine to protect it. On each side of the gullet there is a padded panel that prevents pressure on the horse's spine. A saddle is held in position with a strap, known as a girth or cinch, which fits under the horse's chest and is secured on each side of the saddle by buckles. Stirrups are also attached to the saddle to help the rider balance on and manoeuvre the horse. There are various types of saddle, each modified for a different type of riding. For example, a showjumping saddle has forward-cut flaps to help the rider sit in the correct position for jumping: leaning forwards with the knees bent. A Western saddle is designed for riding for long periods; the saddle seat is padded and the stirrups are long so that the rider can sit in a relaxed position.

RACING SADDLE

Cut-back head

Cantle

Forward-cut flap

Surcingle loop

Rawhide stirrup-leather

Lightweight steel stirrup-iron

Embroidered saddle

Bridle

Embroidered cloth

Tassel

EMBROIDERED SADDLE AND CLOTH ON A HORSE

Cantle

Seat

Pommel

Waist

Skirt

Panel

Stirrup-bar

Leather lining

D-ring

Stirrup-leather keeper

Stirrup-leather

Bridle

Head collar

Stirrup in run-up position

Sheepskin numnah

Rein

Flap

Numbered hole in stirrup-leather

Eggbutt snaffle

Balding leather girth

Atherstone girth

English hunting stirrup-iron

ENGLISH SADDLE ON A HORSE

GENERAL-PURPOSE SADDLE

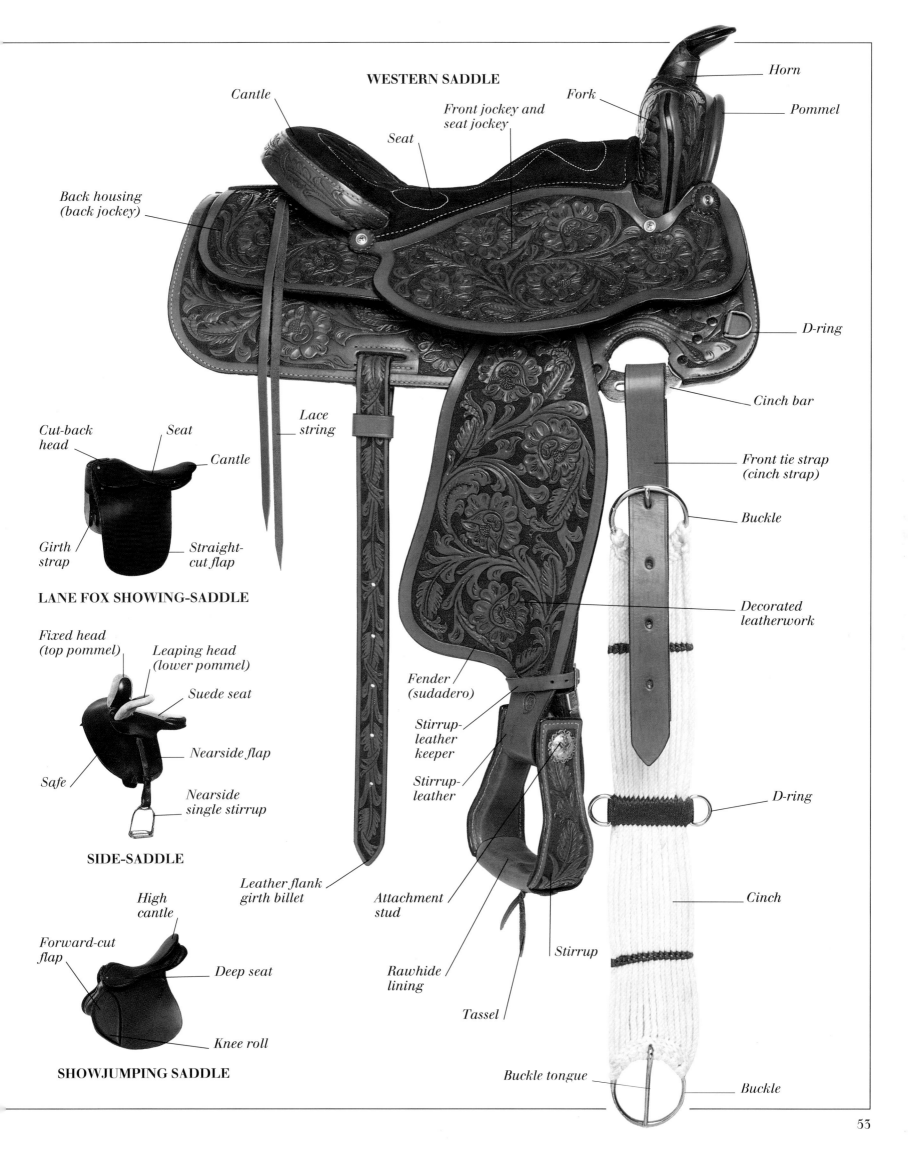

WESTERN SADDLE

Cantle

Front jockey and seat jockey

Seat

Fork

Horn

Pommel

Back housing (back jockey)

D-ring

Lace string

Cinch bar

Front tie strap (cinch strap)

Cut-back head

Seat

Cantle

Girth strap

Straight-cut flap

LANE FOX SHOWING-SADDLE

Buckle

Decorated leatherwork

Fixed head (top pommel)

Leaping head (lower pommel)

Suede seat

Nearside flap

Safe

Nearside single stirrup

SIDE-SADDLE

Fender (sudadero)

Stirrup-leather keeper

Stirrup-leather

D-ring

High cantle

Forward-cut flap

Deep seat

Leather flank girth billet

Attachment stud

Rawhide lining

Stirrup

Cinch

Knee roll

Tassel

SHOWJUMPING SADDLE

Buckle tongue

Buckle

53

Grooming

GROOMING KEEPS THE HORSE'S COAT and hoofs clean and helps to improve the circulation in the skin. During a grooming session, each part of the horse is carefully cleaned. Dirt and debris in the horse's hoofs are picked out with a hoof pick, and the hoofs may be oiled. If the horse is washed, excess water is scraped off the coat with a sweat scraper. If the horse is not washed, surface mud and sweat are brushed off the coat with a stiff-bristled dandy brush. Grease and dust are removed with a soft-bristled body brush that is cleaned every few strokes with a metal curry-comb. Although the metal curry-comb is never used directly on the horse, a plastic curry-comb can be brushed through the coat to remove mud, and a rubber curry-comb used to remove mud and old, shed hair. A cloth called a stable rubber is used to give the coat a final wipe over. The horse's eyes and nostrils are wiped clean with a damp sponge. The mane and tail are brushed thoroughly with a body brush, and the mane may be damped down and brushed to one side with a water brush (known as laying the mane). If the horse is being groomed for a show, the mane and tail may be prepared for plaiting with the mane comb. Patterns may be made on the horse's hindquarters by combing through a template in a different direction to the rest of the coat, creating quarter marks such as shark's teeth or a checker-board. In winter, the horse grows a long coat, which may be clipped to prevent the horse from sweating excessively when being worked or ridden. The coat may be clipped entirely – a full clip – or only partly, as in the hunter clip for example.

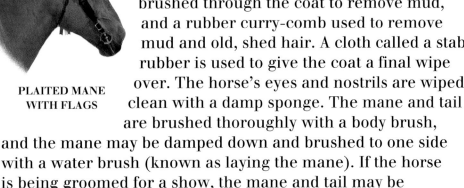

PLAITED MANE
WITH FLAGS

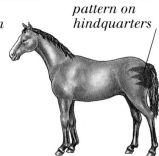

QUARTER MARKS

Checker-board pattern on hindquarters

Shark's teeth pattern on hindquarters

CHECKER-BOARD

SHARK'S TEETH

EXAMPLES OF CLIPS

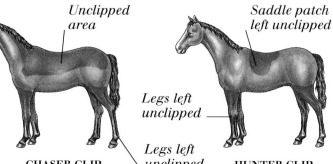

Unclipped area

Saddle patch left unclipped

Legs left unclipped

Legs left unclipped

CHASER CLIP

HUNTER CLIP

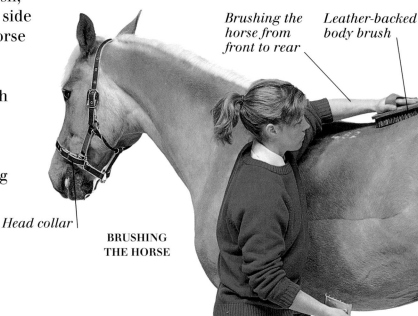

Brushing the horse from front to rear

Leather-backed body brush

Head collar

BRUSHING
THE HORSE

Jodhpurs

Metal curry-comb for cleaning the brush

Rubber riding boots

GROOMING A HORSE

Cleaning the hoof with a hoof pick

PICKING OUT THE FEET

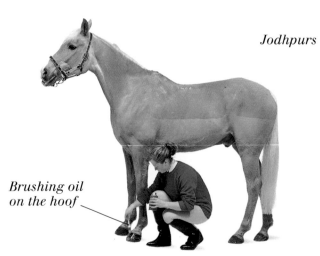

Brushing oil on the hoof

OILING THE HOOFS

GROOMING KIT

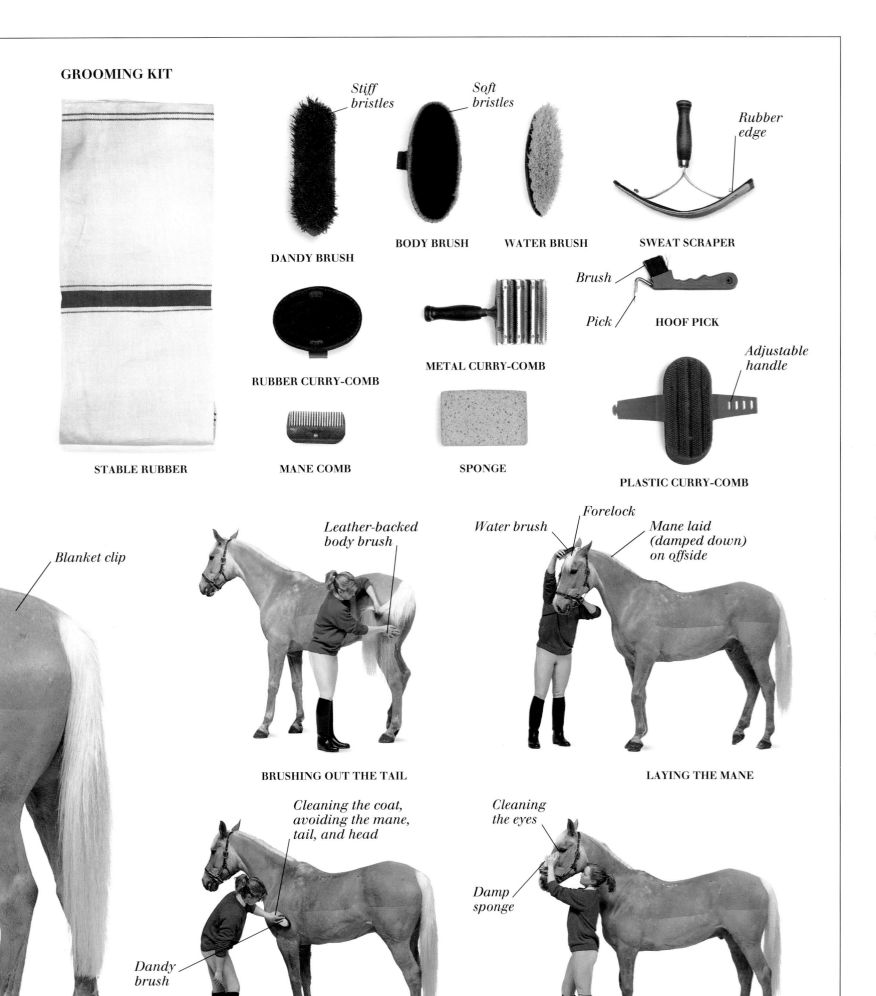

Stiff bristles

Soft bristles

Rubber edge

DANDY BRUSH

BODY BRUSH

WATER BRUSH

SWEAT SCRAPER

Brush

Pick

HOOF PICK

RUBBER CURRY-COMB

METAL CURRY-COMB

Adjustable handle

STABLE RUBBER

MANE COMB

SPONGE

PLASTIC CURRY-COMB

Blanket clip

Leather-backed body brush

Water brush

Forelock

Mane laid (damped down) on offside

BRUSHING OUT THE TAIL

LAYING THE MANE

Cleaning the coat, avoiding the mane, tail, and head

Cleaning the eyes

Damp sponge

Dandy brush

USING THE DANDY BRUSH

SPONGING THE EYES AND NOSTRILS

Shoeing and shoes

A HORSE'S HOOF FORMS A PROTECTIVE COVERING over the sensitive, inner part of the foot. Horses that are ridden or worked without shoes can wear down and damage their hoofs, which may lead to sore feet or even lameness. To prevent injuries, horses are fitted with shoes by a farrier. The shoes are selected for particular functions; for instance, lightweight, aluminium shoes (called racing plates) are worn for racing. To fit a new shoe, the farrier removes the old one and shapes the hoof with a rasp and a knife. The new shoe may then be fixed to the hoof by one of two methods: hot-shoeing or cold-shoeing. In hot-shoeing, the farrier shapes the shoe by heating it in a furnace until it is red-hot and malleable, then hammers the shoe into shape on an anvil. The farrier places the hot shoe on the hoof to burn a mark that acts as a guide for reshaping the shoe. The shoe is repeatedly reheated and reshaped until it fits properly, and then it is nailed to the hoof. The nail-ends are ripped off with a hammer-claw, and the remaining sharp nail-heads are hammered over to form clenches. Finally, the farrier files smooth the clenches with a rasp and trims the hoof. In cold-shoeing, a shoe of the right size is nailed to the hoof without having been repeatedly reheated and reshaped. Racing plates are usually fixed using this method.

SHOES

Plain heel

Sturdy shoe for heavy horses

Lightweight, aluminium shoe for racehorses

PLAIN "STAMPED" SHOE   **RACING PLATE**

Fullering to give riding horses better grip

Pencilled heel

Corrective shoe for navicular disease

FULLERED SHOE   **"EGG-BAR" SURGICAL SHOE**

Farrier files hoof to its normal length, having removed old shoe

Rasp

Hammer

Knife

PREPARING THE HOOF

HOT-SHOEING A HORSE

Furnace

Shoe is heated in furnace to make it malleable

Embers | *Tongs* | *Long-handled pincers*

FORGING (HEATING AND SHAPING) THE SHOE

Overgrown part of hoof is removed, and hoof is trimmed and cleaned

Knife

Hammer

Hammer

Anvil

TRIMMING THE HOOF

Shoe is hammered into shape

Tongs

SHAPING THE SHOE

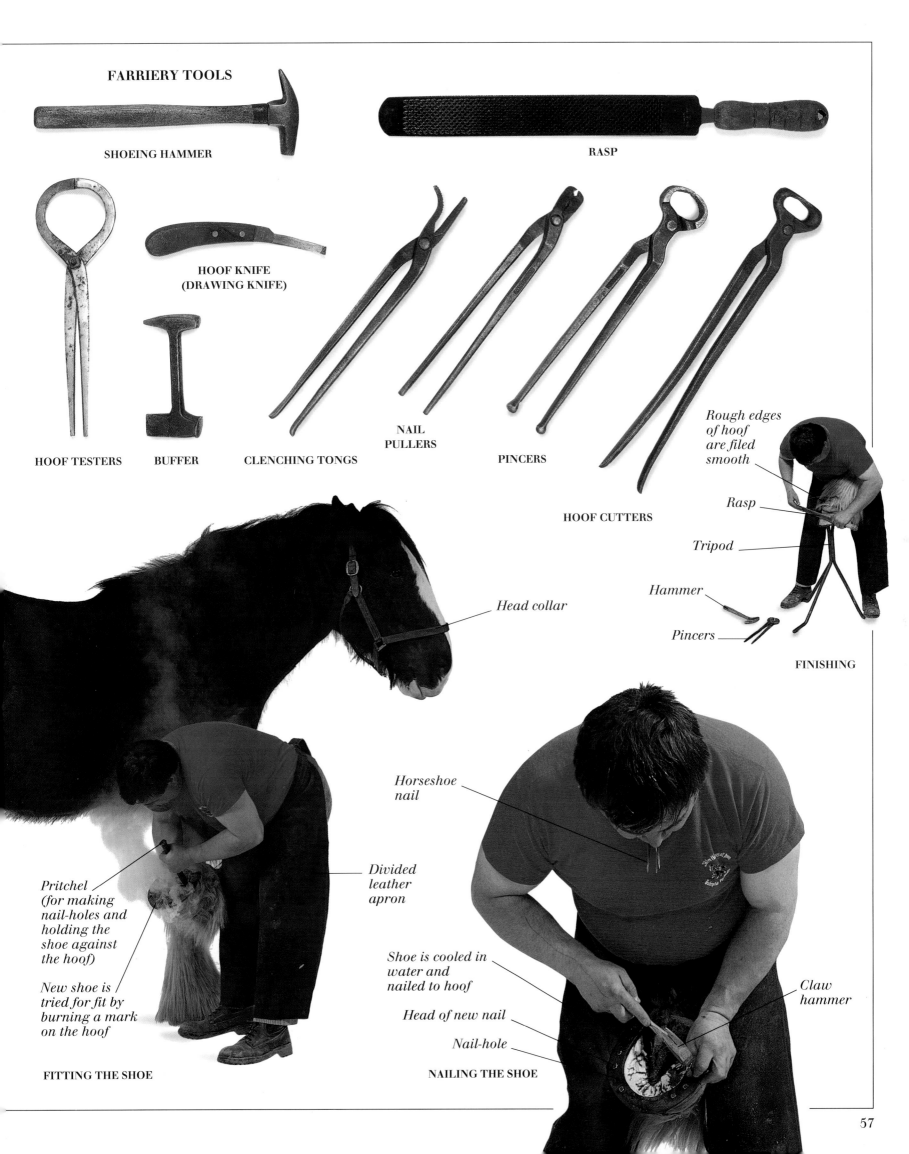

FARRIERY TOOLS

SHOEING HAMMER

RASP

HOOF KNIFE
(DRAWING KNIFE)

HOOF TESTERS

BUFFER

CLENCHING TONGS

NAIL
PULLERS

PINCERS

HOOF CUTTERS

*Rough edges
of hoof
are filed
smooth*

Rasp

Tripod

Hammer

Pincers

FINISHING

Head collar

*Horseshoe
nail*

*Divided
leather
apron*

*Pritchel
(for making
nail-holes and
holding the
shoe against
the hoof)*

*New shoe is
tried for fit by
burning a mark
on the hoof*

FITTING THE SHOE

*Shoe is cooled in
water and
nailed to hoof*

Head of new nail

Nail-hole

*Claw
hammer*

NAILING THE SHOE

57

Horse family

HORSES, ASSES, AND ZEBRAS belong to a single family of mammals called the Equidae, the present-day members of which are shown below. The Equidae form part of a larger grouping called the Perissodactyla, which also includes rhinoceroses. Perissodactyls typically have either one or three digits on each limb; equids have one digit. In the wild, equids feed by grazing on grasses and shrubs, live in open country, and are fast-running animals that depend on speed to escape predators. They are highly social animals, living in large herds, each consisting of several family groups. All equids can interbreed to produce hybrids. For example, a male donkey mated with a female horse produces a mule. Most hybrids are sterile and therefore cannot have offspring.

EXAMPLES OF HYBRIDS

Male donkey	+	Female horse	=	Mule
Female donkey	+	Male horse	=	Hinny; jennet
Zebra	+	Horse	=	Zebroid
Zebra	+	Donkey	=	Zedonk

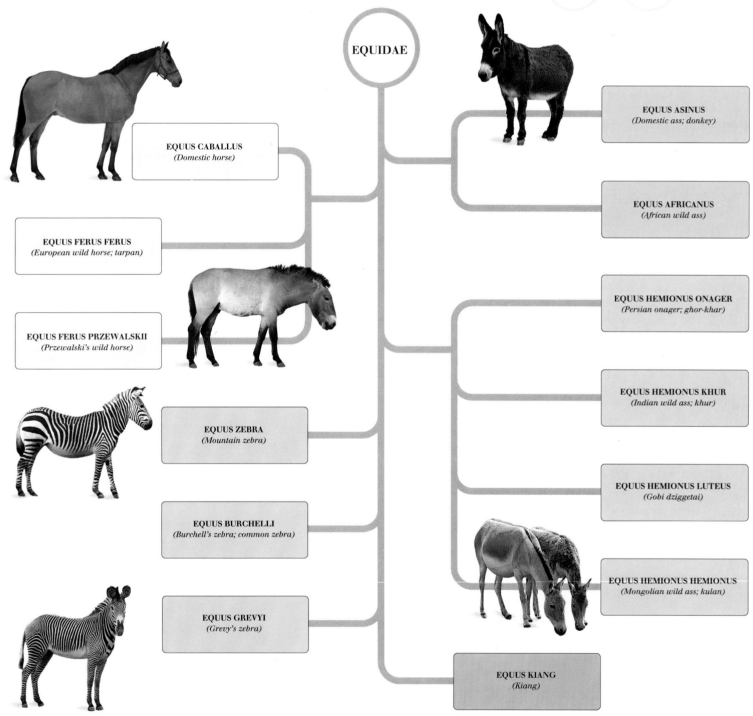

EQUIDAE

EQUUS CABALLUS
(Domestic horse)

EQUUS FERUS FERUS
(European wild horse; tarpan)

EQUUS FERUS PRZEWALSKII
(Przewalski's wild horse)

EQUUS ZEBRA
(Mountain zebra)

EQUUS BURCHELLI
(Burchell's zebra; common zebra)

EQUUS GREVYI
(Grevy's zebra)

EQUUS ASINUS
(Domestic ass; donkey)

EQUUS AFRICANUS
(African wild ass)

EQUUS HEMIONUS ONAGER
(Persian onager; ghor-khar)

EQUUS HEMIONUS KHUR
(Indian wild ass; khur)

EQUUS HEMIONUS LUTEUS
(Gobi dziggetai)

EQUUS HEMIONUS HEMIONUS
(Mongolian wild ass; kulan)

EQUUS KIANG
(Kiang)

Glossary

AGED: A horse that is seven or more years old.

AIDS: The means by which the rider or driver communicates his or her instructions to the horse. **Natural aids** include legs, hands, seat, and voice. **Artificial aids** include whips, spurs, and martingales. (See also Martingale.)

ASS: A member of the Equidae. The two existing groups of wild asses are the Asian wild ass and the African wild ass. (See also Equidae.)

BIT: The part of the bridle that is fitted into the horse's mouth over the tongue. Bits are made of metal, although the mouthpiece may be covered in rubber or vulcanite. The mouthpiece may be straight, mullen (half-moon), or ported (with a hump in the middle). There are various types of bits, including snaffle, pelham, and curb bits. (See also Bridle.)

BLINKERS: Leather flaps attached to the bridle, used to prevent a horse from seeing anywhere other than in front. (See also Bridle.)

BREAKING-IN: The initial training of a horse for riding or harness work.

BREECHING: The part of a harness that enables a horse to brake or reverse when pulling a load.

BREED: An equine group that has been bred selectively for consistent characteristics over a long period of time. A true breed will be registered in a stud book. (See also Stud book.)

BRIDLE: The part of a horse's tack that is used to regulate the position of the horse's head, and to help control the pace and direction of the horse. There are various types of bridles, including double, snaffle, and Western bridles. (See also Tack.)

BRIDOON: A snaffle bit that is used with a curb bit on a double bridle. (See also Bit; Bridle.)

CANNON BONE: A bone in a horse's leg. In the foreleg the cannon bone is between the knee and the fetlock. In the hind leg the cannon bone is between the hock and the fetlock.

CANTER: One of the horse's natural gaits. It is faster than the walk and the trot, but slower than the gallop.

CHESTNUT: The horny, oval pad found on the inner side of the forelegs, and on the inner side of the hocks on the hind legs. The term chestnut is also used to describe a reddish-gold coat colour.

COLLAR: The part of a harness that enables a horse to pull a load. The collar is oval, often made of wood, and covered in leather.

COLT: An ungelded male horse less than four years old. (See also Gelding.)

CONFORMATION: The overall external physical structure of a horse.

CRUPPER: A leather strap that helps keep the saddle or pad in place, preventing it from sliding forwards over the horse's withers.

DANDY BRUSH: A brush used to remove mud and sweat from a horse's coat.

DONKEY: A member of the Equidae. The donkey is a domesticated ass descended from the African wild ass. (See also Equidae.)

DORSAL STRIPE: A band of black hairs that extends along a horse's back.

EQUIDAE: A family of mammals consisting of horses, wild asses, domesticated asses (donkeys), and zebras.

ERGOT: A small, horny patch behind the fetlocks.

FARRIER: A person who makes horseshoes and shoes horses.

FEATHER: Long hair on the lower part of the legs, particularly around the fetlocks. Heavy horses often have feathered legs. (See also Heavy horse.)

FILLY: A female horse less than four years old.

FLAT-RACE: A horse-race in which horses race over a course without jumps.

FOAL: A horse less than one year old.

FROG: The V-shaped, horny pad on the bottom of a horse's foot that acts as a shock absorber.

FULLERED SHOE: A horseshoe with a groove hollowed out along its surface. The groove makes the shoe lighter and gives the horse better grip.

GAIT (PACES): The way in which a horse moves. The horse has four natural gaits: walk, trot, canter, and gallop. A horse can also be trained to do specialized gaits, such as pacing. (See also Canter; Gallop; Trot; Walk.)

GALLOP: The fastest of the horse's natural gaits.

GALVAYNE'S GROOVE: A groove that appears on the upper corner incisors and which can be used to determine the age of a horse.

GELDING: A castrated male horse. Stallions that are not suitable for stud purposes are often gelded to make them easier to manage.

GIRTH: The circumference of a horse, measured behind the withers and around the deepest part of the body. The term girth is also used for a strap, usually made of leather, webbing, or nylon, that passes under the body to hold the saddle in place.

HALTER: A set of straps with lead rope attached, used for leading or tying a horse that is not wearing a bridle.

HAND: A unit of measurement used to describe a horse's height (which is measured from the highest point of the withers). One hand equals four inches (about 10 cm). Subdivisions of the hand are expressed in inches: thus 14.2 hands is 14 hands and 2 inches (147 cm). (See also Withers.)

HARNESS: The equipment that enables a horse to pull a load. Harnesses usually consist of a bridle, collar, and breeching. (See also Breeching; Bridle; Collar.)

HEAVY HORSE: A large, powerful horse that has been used in agriculture and for hauling heavy loads. Heavy horses typically stand between 14.2 and 18 hands (147–183 cm) high.

HINDQUARTERS: The part of the horse's body from the rear of the flank to the dock of the tail, as far down as the top of the gaskin on the hind legs.

HINNY (JENNET): The offspring of a male horse and a female donkey.

HURDLE-RACE: A horse-race in which horses race over a course with jumps that are 107 cm (3 ft 6 in) high and over.

LIGHT HORSE: Any horse, other than a heavy horse or pony, whose size and conformation make it suitable for riding or driving. Light horses typically stand between 14.2 and 17.2 hands (147–178 cm) high.

MARE: A female horse more than four years old.

MARTINGALE: A strap, or set of straps, used to prevent the horse pulling its head too high. The two most common types are the **running martingale** and the **standing martingale**. A third type of martingale, the **Irish martingale**, is used almost exclusively in racing to prevent the reins from flying over the horse's head in the event of a fall.

MULE: The offspring of a male donkey and a female horse.

NEARSIDE: The left side of a horse. This is the side from which it is usual to mount and dismount as well as to lead the horse and to tack up. (See also Offside.)

NUMNAH: A pad placed under the saddle to prevent undue pressure, rubbing, and chafing on the horse's back.

OFFSIDE: The right side of a horse. (See also Nearside.)

PEDIGREE: The record of ancestry of a horse. Pedigree must be proven in order to be entered into a breed society stud book. (See also Stud book.)

POINTS: The visible external features of a horse, such as the withers, as well as the parts of the skeleton and the superficial muscles that can be felt through the skin.

PONY: Any horse that is 14.2 hands (147 cm) or less in height.

QUARTER MARKS: Decorative patterns on a horse's hindquarters made by brushing through a template in a different direction to the rest of the coat.

SILKS: The jacket and cap worn by a jockey in racing. Each set of silks has a particular pattern and colour combination that are used to identify the horse's owner.

STALLION: An ungelded male horse more than four years old.

STEEPLECHASE: A horse-race in which horses race over a course with jumps that are 137 cm (4 ft 6 in) high and over.

STIFLE: The joint between the lower end of the femur and the upper end of the tibia and fibula.

STIRRUP-IRON: A loop, ring, or similar device suspended from a saddle to support the rider's foot. Stirrup-irons are made of metal, usually stainless steel.

STUD BOOK: The book kept by a breed society in which the pedigrees of pure-bred stock are recorded.

SULKY: A lightweight, two-wheeled cart used in harness racing.

SURCINGLE: A belt that is used to keep a rug or saddle in place.

SURGICAL SHOE: Any of various special types of shoe used to correct diseases or deformities of the hoof.

TACK: A general term covering all saddlery and harness equipment.

THROATLATCH: A leather strap that is a part of the bridle. It passes around a horse's cheeks and under its throat. The throatlatch prevents the bridle from being pulled off over the horse's ears in the event of a fall. (See also Bridle.)

TROT: One of the horse's natural gaits. It is faster than the walk but slower than the canter and gallop.

TYPE: A horse that fulfils a specific purpose but does not necessarily belong to a specific breed. For example, a hunter is a riding horse that is used specifically for hunting. (See also Breed.)

WALK: The slowest of the horse's natural gaits.

WITHERS: The part of the horse at the base of the neck, where the neck joins the body, above the shoulders.

YEARLING: A horse of either sex, from the age of one year.

ZEBROID: The offspring of a zebra and a horse.

ZEDONK: The offspring of a zebra and a donkey.

Index

Acknowledgments

Dorling Kindersley would like to thank:
Brian Crane AFCL Farrier, New Barnet, Hertfordshire, UK; the Whitbread Hop Farm, Paddock Wood, Kent, UK; James Fanshawe; the Royal Veterinary College, London, UK; Jockey Club Estates Limited, UK; the National Shire Horse Centre, Plymouth, Devon, UK; W. H. Gidden Ltd, London, UK; the Marwell Zoological Park, Winchester, Hampshire, UK; Pauline Jones and Jaffa, owned by Mrs Bonner

Picture credits:
2c, 6cl Thoroughbred - *Lyphento*, Conkwell Grange Stud, Avon, UK; 8bl Orlov Trotter - Moscow Hippodrome, Russian Federation; 8br, 8cr Pinto - *Hit Man*, Boyd Cantrell, Kentucky Horse Park, USA; 2cr and 8cl Gelderlander - *Spooks*, Peter Munt, Ascot Driving Stables, Berkshire, UK; 6-7main, 7br, 8tc Danish Warmblood - *Rambo*, Jorgen Olsen, Denmark; 9tl Connemara - *Spinway Bright Morning*, Miss S. Hodgkins, Spinway Stud, Oxfordshire, UK; 9tc, 4l Lusitano - *Montemere-O-Nova*, Nan Thurman, Turville Valley Stud, Oxfordshire, UK; 9cl Palomino - *Wychwood Dynascha*, Mrs G. Harwood, Wychwood Stud, Gloucestershire, UK; 9cr Friesian - *Sjouke*, Sonia Gray, Tattondale Carriages, Cheshire, UK; 9cl Camargue - *Redounet*, Mr Contreras, Les Saintes Maries de la Mer, France; 9bl Holstein - *Lenard*, Sue Watson, Trenawin Stud, Cornwall, UK; 9br Appaloosa - *Golden Nugget*, Sally Chaplin, Oxfordshire, UK; 28tl Falabella - *Pegasus of Kilverstone*, Lady Fisher, Kilverstone Wildlife Park, Norfolk, UK; 28bl New Forest pony - *Bowerwood Aquila*, Mrs Rae Turner, Bowerwood Stud, Hampshire, UK; 28tr American Shetland pony - *Little Trouble*, Marvin McCabe, Kentucky Horse Park, USA; 28cr Bardigiano - *Pippo*, Istituto Incremento Ippico di Crema, Italy; 28-29b Fjord pony - *Ausdan Svejk*, John Goddard Fenwick and Lyn Moran, Ausdan Stud, Dyfed, UK; 29tl Rocky Mountain pony - *Mocha Monday*, Rea Swan, Hope Springs Farm, Kentucky Horse Park, USA; 29tc Welsh pony - *Twyford Signal*, Mr and Mrs L. E. Bigley, Llanarth Stud, Hereford, UK; 29tr, 8tl Highland pony - *Fruich of Dykes*, Countess of Swinton, UK; 29cl Bashkir - *Mel's Lucky Boy*, Dan Stewart Family, Kentucky Horse Park, USA; 29c Dales pony - *Warrenlane Duke*, Mr Dickson, Millbeck Pony Stud, Yorkshire, UK; 29br, 4r Dartmoor pony - *Allendale Vampire*, Miss M. Houlden, Haven Stud, Hereford, UK; 30tl Icelandic horse - *Leiknir*, Kentucky Horse Farm, USA; 30cl, 6tl Exmoor pony - *Murrayton Delphinus*, June Freeman, Murrayton Stud, Hertfordshire, UK; 30bl Fell pony - *Waverhead William*, Mr and Mrs S. Errington, UK; 30br Welsh Mountain pony - *Bengad Dark Mullein*, Mrs C. Bowyer, Symondsbury Stud,

Sussex, UK; 30-31main Australian pony - *Malibu Park Command Performance*, K. and L. Sinclair, Victoria, Australia; 31tl Caspian pony - *Hopstone Shabdiz*, Mrs Scott, Henden Caspian Stud, Wiltshire, UK; 31tr Haflinger pony - *Nomad*, Miss Helen Blair, Silvretta Haflinger Stud, West Midlands, UK; 31cr Pottock pony - *Thouarec III*, Haras National de Tarbes, France; 31cl Ariègeois pony - *Radium*, Haras National de Pau, France; 31bl Hackney pony - *Hurstwood Consort*, Mr and Mrs Hayden, Hurstwood Stud, UK; 31br, 8cr Landais pony - *Hippolyte*, Haras National de Pau, France; 32bl, 9bc Frederiksborg - *Zarif Langløkkegard*, Harry Nielsen, Denmark; 32cr, 9tr Cleveland Bay - *Oaten Mainbrace*, Mr and Mrs Dimmock; 32br Lipizzaner - *Siglavy Szella*, John Goddard Fenwick and Lyn Moran; 32-33main Hanoverian - *Défilante*, Barry Mawdsley, European Horse Enterprises, Berkshire, UK; 33tl Tennessee Walking horse - *Delight's Moondust*, Andrew and Jane Shaw, Kentucky Horse Park, USA; 33tc Morgan - *Fox Creek's Dynasty*, Darwin Olsen, Kentucky Horse Park, USA; 33cr, 2tr, 8tr Quarter-horse - *Doc's Maharajah*, Harold Bush, Kentucky Horse Park, USA; 33br Standardbred - *Rambling Willie*, Farrington Stables and Estate of Paul Siebert, Kentucky Horse Park, USA; 34tl Arab - *Muskhari Silver*, Janet and Anne Connolly, Silver Fox Arabians, West Midlands, UK; 34tr Akhal-Teke - *Fakir-Bola*, Moscow Hippodrome, Russian Federation; 34cr Kabardin - Moscow Hippodrome, Russian Federation; 34br Barb - *Taw's Little Buck*, Kentucky Horse Park, USA; 2bl and 34cl Shagya-Arab - *Artaxerxes*, Jeanette Bauch and Jens Brinksten, Denmark; 34bl and 4r Anglo-Arab - *Restif*, Haras National De Compiègne, France; 35tl Don - *Baret*, Moscow Hippodrome, Russian Federation; 35tc Trakehner - *Muschamp Mauersee*, Janet Lorch, Muschamp Stud, Buckinghamshire, UK; 35tr Budenny - *Barin*, Moscow Hippodrome, Russian Federation; 35c Nonius - *Pampas*, A. G. Kishumseigi, Hungary; 2cr, 8cl, 35cr Dutch Warmblood - *Edison*, Mrs Dejonge; 35cl French Trotter - *Pur Historien*, Haras National De Compiègne, France; 35bl Selle Français - *Prince D'elle*, Haras Natonal De Saint Lô, France; 35br, 5cl Andalucian - *Campanero XXIV*, Nigel Oliver, Singleborough Stud, Buckinghamshire, UK; 36tl, 54tl Suffolk Punch - *Laurel Keepsake II*, P. Adams and Sons; 36bl Clydesdale - *Blue Print*, Mervyn and Pauline Ramage, Mount Farm, Clydesdale horses, Tyne and Wear, UK; 36-37main Shire - *Duke*, Jim Lockwood, Courage Shire Horse Centre, Buckinghamshire, UK; 37tr, 4c Breton - *Ulysses*, Haras National de Tarbes, France; 37cr Boulonnais -

Urus, Haras National de Compiègne, France; 37cr Norman Cob - *Ibis*, Haras National de Saint Lô, France; 37cl Brabant - *Roy*, Kentucky Horse Park, USA; 37br Jutland - *Tempo*, Jørgen Neilsen, Denmark; 37bl Italian Heavy Draught - *Nobile*, Istituto Incremento Ippico di Crema, Italy; 38tl Russian Heavy Draught - *Bespechny*, Moscow Agricultural Academy, Russian Federation; 38cl Vladmir Heavy Draught - *Vostorg*, Central Moscow Hippodrome, Russian Federation; 38c Murakozer - *Baba*, Kobza Istvan; 38cr North Swedish horse - *Ysterman*, Ingvar Andersson, Sweden; 38bl Dutch Draught - *Marquis van de Lindenhoeve*, Albert ter wal; 38bc Comtois - *Attila*, Haras de Pau, France; 38br Poitevin - *Vitrisse*, Haras National de la Roche sur yon, France; 6bl, 38-39main Percheron - *Tango*, Haras National de Saint Lô, France; 39tr, 9c, 4l Ardennais - *Ramses du Vallon*, Haras National de Pau, France; 58tl Riding pony - *Brutt*, Robert Oliver

Photography:
Dave King 1; Steve Gorton 5br, 52br, 53r; Andy Crawford 3c, 46tr, 47t, 48-49; Dave Rudkin 2tc, 2br, 5tl, 44, 45main, 45tr, 51r, 52tr; Tim Ridley 12, 13main, 13tr, 50r, 51tl, 51tc, 53tl, 53cl, 53bl; Colin Keates of the Natural History Museum 10, 11main, 14bl, 14br, 15bl, 15br; Gordon Clayton 5tr, 26bl, 26bc, 26br, 27bl, 27br; Jerry Young 26tl, 43b, 44b, 52tl, 56tl, 56bl, 56br, 56cr, 56-57main, 57br, 57cr, 58tr, 58br, 58cl, 58bl, 58bcl; Bob Langrish 5cr, 40-41main, 42tl; Karl Shone 46-47main, 51cl; Bruce Coleman Limited/Jane Burton 27tr; Anna Hodgson 56tr, 57t; Peter Chadwick 50tl, 51bl, 52bl, 54bl, 54bc, 54-55main, 55cl, 55bl, 55cr, 55br; Stephen Oliver 8br, 50l

(t=top, b=bottom, l=left, r=right, c=centre)

Picture research:
Joanna Thomas

Additional illustrations:
Roy Flooks; Selwyn Hutchinson; Simone End; John Temperton; Sandra Pond and Will Giles

Additional editorial assistance:
Geoffrey Stalker; Liz Wheeler

Index:
Susan Bosanko